As Knowing Goes

AS KNOWING GOES

and Other Poems

Christopher Norris

Parlor Press
Anderson, South Carolina
www.parlorpress.com

Parlor Press LLC, Anderson, South Carolina, 29621

© 2022 by Parlor Press
All rights reserved.
Printed in the United States of America
S A N: 2 5 4 - 8 8 7 9

Library of Congress Cataloging-in-Publication Data on File

978-1-64317-258-3 (paperback)
978-1-64317-259-0 (PDF)
978-1-64317-260-6 (ePub)

1 2 3 4 5

Cover design by David Blakesley.
Cover art: "Arrival of the Normandy Train, Gare Saint-Lazare"
 by Claude Monet. 1877. Oil on canvas. Mr. and Mrs.
  Martin A. Ryerson Collection, The Art Institute of Chicago
Printed on acid-free paper.

Parlor Press, LLC is an independent publisher of scholarly and trade titles in print and multimedia formats. This book is available in paperback and ebook formats from Parlor Press on the World Wide Web at http://www.parlorpress.com or through online and brick-and-mortar bookstores. For submission information or to find out about Parlor Press publications, write to Parlor Press, 3015 Brackenberry Drive, Anderson, South Carolina, 29621, or email editor@parlorpress.com.

For Clare, Jenny, Dylan, Avery, and Arlo

Le moi est haïssable.
　　　　Blaise Pascal, *Pensées*

Contents

Foreword ix
Acknowledgments xvi

   As Knowing Goes *1*
   End-Time *3*
   Odysseus at Forty *5*
   Material: A Sonnet *11*
   Ancrene Wisse *12*
   Negentropes: Two Poems *16*
   Endolphins *19*
   An Eton Mess *21*
   Rank-Shifting: An Allegory *23*
   Another Journey *25*
   Diamantine: an exchange *36*
   After Lockdown *40*
   Tampering *43*
   Clocks: A Villanelle *47*
   A Wild Analysis *48*
   Thing *52*
   Martyrs of Coal *54*
   For Mike Billinton (1933–2019) *56*
   These Fuellish Things *58*
   Priorities *60*
   Bertolt Brecht: Advice to Lyric Poets *63*
   Tyche's Share *67*
   Fixers: Post-Election Thoughts *70*
   The Eliot File *73*
   Measure *78*
   Love Foresworn *84*
   Vermin *86*

Elements *93*
Life and Logic: An Agon (Frege) *98*
Politics and Poetry: two views *101*
Après-Coup *103*
Rhyme and Rote: A Caesurelle *108*
Macaque *111*
Ernesto Cardenal (1925–2020) *113*
Two Books *115*
Grieve for Me Piecemeal *117*
Zoom: Four Predicaments *119*
Exits: Double Whammy *124*
Buckling *126*
Villon to Petrarch: a Flyting *131*
Coronavirus: Retrospect 2040 *134*
Ruins *138*
Waves *140*
Sonnet: after Horace *149*
About the Author 151

Foreword

These poems were written during the period 2018-2021 and some of them bear witness to its hectic, politically divisive and often tumultuous character. Others fall under a range of generic descriptors such as verse-essay, verse-epistle, meditation, elegy, lyric (non-confessional), song, anthem (secular), dramatic monologue, verse-dialogue, satire, polemic, and lament. They are, with just one exception, pointedly 'formalist' in the sense that they deploy — and delight in deploying — rhyme and meter along with a great many verse-forms, structures and prosodic devices by way of getting their point across. I should add that they do indeed have various sorts of point and do make a virtue of clear communication. That is, they imply (or implicate) a reader who comes to them with intellectual as well as emotional faculties fully engaged and who doesn't, as with so much contemporary verse, allow feeling to subdue any active concern with their formal and thematic aspects.

I included 'lyric' among the genres represented but had better say more precisely what I mean by that term. Lyric has been the predominant mode in English-language poetry since the Romantic period and had occupied a prominent place in that tradition from the Renaissance down. What changed most markedly with the advent of Romanticism was the increased emphasis on first-person utterance and, closely related to that, the implicit claim to be speaking, expressing, or directly manifesting the poet's experience (often of love whether new-found or lost) and her/his feelings about it. In so far as poetry readers keep up with developments in literary theory they will be aware that some caution is required in such matters, especially as concerns not being so naïve as to take that claim at face value. Probably the pertinent distinctions are better grasped by readers of fiction where terms like 'author', 'implied author', and 'narrator' have achieved a degree of popular currency, along with 'focalizer' for the technically-minded. But they also have their place in the reading of poetry where confusion as to *qui parle ici?* can give rise to some bad misunderstandings. Some 'lyric' poems here can be taken, by and large, as first-person expressions of feeling, thought or experience (though always, as Wordsworth wisely pointed out, 'recollected in tranquility'). Other pieces range from oblique or mediated self-reference to vicarious projection, counterfactual conjecture, apotropaic self-defense (spot those if you will!), and fictive role-playing.

For what it's worth my experience is that poems justifiably described as 'lyric' may take rise from, and start out by expressing, a variety of moods (very often melancholic) but then go on — in what feels more like a third-person voice — to explore them reflectively by way of imagery and metaphor. At any rate the focus can shift a good deal and the process is one that very easily extends to the point where longer lyric forms move over generically into the mode of dramatic monologue. One clear benefit of formalism is that it does draw attention, through various prosodic and structural devices, to the element of craft or creative-constructive 'making' that went into a lyric poem's often quite lengthy and complicated process of production. The one exception here to my formalist *parti pris* is 'Another Journey' where the mode is 'free verse' (an oxymoron if ever there was one!) but where the reader should soon detect the presence of a basically four-stress rhythmic pattern. The poem has a lot to do with T.S. Eliot's long-lasting and, I would say, far from benign influence on present-day thinking about poetry, culture, religion, and politics. That influence has been exerted in large part — so the poem suggests — through a strangely compelling though somnolent verse-music with its own designs on the suitably attuned or pre-adjusted reader. This goes along with other marked attributes of Eliot's poetry: its imagist suppression of discursive thought, its heavy reliance on free-associative linkage as a source of thematic coherence, and its exploitation (the word seems appropriate) of mythic, metaphorical or symbolist devices, some of which nudge that reader toward decidedly murky psycho-sexual-cultural-political regions. The rise of large-scale, institutionally sanctioned stupidity has been among the most depressing aspects of recent Anglo-US history and one that has found an equally depressing equivalent in poetry's failure, by and large, to engage actively with its varied manifestations.

What most needs reviving in order to resist this widespread retreat is a poetry that combines exacting formal standards with commitment to the values of intelligence, critique and (not least) responsiveness to urgent social and political issues. 'Articulate energy' — Donald Davie's book title is one I would happily adopt as a working manifesto, along with large parts of the elective prehistory in verse-practice that he offers by way of genealogical warrant. That a poem can have the required kind of affective or emotional 'energy' while deploying a wide range of formal resources — both prosodic and (crucially) logico-syntactic — is Davie's conviction and one for which I hope to have provided a decent show of evidence here. It is and has long been, at least since the highpoint of literary Modernism, an unfashionable way of thinking about poetry or even about the novel. On the Modernist account such thinking ignores poetry's autonomous mode of being, its irreducibility to prose paraphrase, its unconcern with ideas or arguments, and its complete isolation from 'extraneous' concerns like history, biography, or politics. These vetoes operate as doctrinal barriers erected around poems by formalist critics of the narrower, more dogmatic and prescriptive 'words-on-the-page' variety. It tends to work best with the sorts of verse produced either by university poets-in-residence and creative-writing teachers or else by first-person lyricists, at any rate those whose intensely private-confessional writing lends itself to treatment in just that hermetically sealed-off manner. Otherwise it has had some observably bad effects, not least by spawning its reactive counterpart in the sorts of 'performance poetry' (not all of it) that make a polemical point of eschewing any least concern with formal matters.

'A plague on both your houses' is no very positive frame of mind in which to proceed so let me set out a few basic tenets. They are, in no single or definite order of importance: that poems are very much in and of the world; that they can and should traffic in ideas, concepts and debates of various sorts; that propositional content, or having a case to put, is no bad thing; that they should possess a major share of the virtues possessed by good, clear-headed prose plus distinctive formal virtues of their own; that to paraphrase a poem is not, as the New Critics preached, a downright 'heresy' but a useful starting-point for getting at those special virtues; and that we do a large disservice to many poems by applying the criteria or modes of readerly engagement encouraged by the programmatic denial of these broad principles. No doubt there is dogmatism here also but at least it may help to shift readers brought up on the regnant Romantic-Imagist-Modernist orthodoxy toward a more open-minded, tolerant view of what contemporary verse can or should be. The poems mostly come with epigraphs or headnotes to offer some help with recondite ideas, out-of-the-way sources, or (in a few cases) associative links that need spelling out. These can best be regarded as parergonal in the sense that Derrida teases from Kantian aesthetics, that is, as being undecidably both inside and outside, integral and separate, a part of and apart from the poem. Like the other 'heresies' of paraphrase, biography, appeals to authorial intention, and so forth, the objection to poetry with notes attached is yet another variant of 'old' New Critical orthodoxy that is long overdue for some creative as well as critical debunking.

One valid aim for poets is to find new and formally inventive ways of combining verse-music with ideas worked out through the thought-provoking interplay of metrical, rhythmic and (not least) syntactic elements. Again these are possibilities that tend to be actively suppressed by such dominant movements or influences in recent poetry as Symbolism, Modernism, Imagism, or indeed New Criticism with its exclusionist stress on inwrought structures of metaphor, irony, or paradox. Their effect is to quarantine poems within a safety-zone intended to set aside matters of philosophical, political, or broader intellectual import. In conjunction with the prevalence of lyric and the widespread rejection of formalism in any guise it very often produces a poetry confined to solitary brooding over private mind-states or inert image-complexes that well-nigh exclude the possibility of discursive thought. Commentators on literary modernism and its aftermath often cite the words of Stein from Conrad's *Lord Jim*: 'in the destructive element immerse.' Substituting 'discursive' for 'destructive' would not fully capture what these poems try to do but may give some idea of their corrective intent.

Thus I cannot, in all conscience, recommend this volume to readers for whom poetry serves chiefly as a confessional outlet, a place of emotional refuge, or a safety-valve for feelings too charged and confused to find more articulate expression. On the other hand, as Eliot said, 'only those who have personality and emotions know what it is to want to escape from these things.' I don't wish to bank too heavily on Eliot's authority here since much of what I have said concerning the negative impact of recent orthodoxies, creative and critical, may be taken as referring to his massive impact on developments in Anglo-American poetry over the past eight decades. That influence has extended to poets who would be anxious to deny it, and to schools and movements across some otherwise sizeable divergences of creed. Among its consequences has been a tendency nowadays to think of 'philosophical poetry' — often with Eliot in mind, especially his late 'Four Quartets' — as involving a suspension of logical thought or discursive rationality, as if this were pretty much required in order for the phrase not to seem an oxymoron.

Hence, as I have said, the Eliotic turn toward symbol, analogy, diffusive metaphor, vaguely evocative sensuous imagery, and a high-toned mystical-religious dimension that draws constantly on just those resources for its power to convince or persuade. Recent studies, by Frank Kermode among others, have tended to identify the major change in his thinking about poetry and religion with Eliot's switch of primary allegiance from Donne and his contemporaries to Dante, the latter now treated as supreme exemplar of the 'unified sensibility' that characterised late-medieval and early Renaissance Christian culture. My belief — in short — is that he would have done much better to stick with Shakespeare, Webster, and Donne rather than sacrifice their most distinctive traits (verbal agility, intellectual acumen, far-reaching curiosity) to a vaguely expressed and highly conservative theocentric worldview. Though many readers find spiritual depth and solace in 'Four Quartets' it is arguable that the virtues in question can at times have more dubious uses, relating as they do to some of Eliot's right-wing religiously and/or racially-motivated views. (See 'Another Journey' and 'The Eliot File' for a more extended verse engagement with some of these issues.) Feelings had better be somewhere within reach of intelligent reflective and self-critical thought, while 'escaping' from feelings — as he crypto-confessionally puts it — might better take the form (as so often in Empson's poetry) of thinking them through in the distinctive ways that formalism offers. In the process they are likely to communicate more effectively — and generate a verse-music of greater complexity and depth — than the boomy echo-chambers of private emotion inhabited by so much contemporary poetry.

Perhaps it needs saying that by 'verse-music' I mean something more than ear-beguiling sounds or the kind of writing that makes up in vocalic-consonantal skill for what it lacks in precisely such complexity and depth. The music of poetry has to do with an intimate linkage between sound, syntax, meter, speech-rhythm, and the subtle interactions of 'content' and 'form' — or sense and structure — that, as most critics agree, should give pause to anyone who cites that distinction. It can be a fairly rough music at times, as was held against Donne and others of his school by critics from Ben Jonson to Samuel Johnson and beyond. What they chiefly objected to was those poets' vexatious combination of 'conceited' (ingenious and challenging) ideas with elaborate syntax, plentiful enjambment, and striking effects of rhythmic irregularity within certain strongly implied metrical norms. These are some of the resources that have been largely thrown away by much present-day poetic practice and I think they are well worth retrieving.

Clive James made some related points in a *TLS* review (August 10th 2001) that, handily enough, took time off to write about Empson's poetry while reviewing a book by Kermode.

> Empson chose to be difficult. He made things difficult for himself with Continental rhyme-schemes fiercely demanding in a rhyme-poor language like English; and he made things difficult for the reader by deploying a range of reference beyond any imaginable single encyclopaedia. Kermode is well equipped to follow up the references, but he makes sure always to follow them in a circle, so that you end up at what really matters about Empson: the compulsively memorable, singing lines whose simplicity the complication is there to protect. The protection was against himself. An appeal for sympathy would have cheapened his feelings, so he put the feelings almost beyond appreciation, as a beggar selling matches might paint a miniature on every box and price them at a thousand pounds each.

My poems make no claim to Empsonian breadth of reference, depth of implication, intellectual wit or haunting musicality. They are boxes with matches that I hope will light in all weathers but of which, to cite Empson in his poem 'This Last Pain', 'most emporia will stock our measure.' Still it is those qualities, so well caught by James and Kermode, that made such a strong impression on me when I first read his poetry as an undergraduate and that I first learned to appreciate in other poets through Empson's criticism. *Pace* Harold Bloom there are some influences that give rise not so much to anxiety, inhibition or hard-won psychic-creative survival but to a long and steadily deepening process of engagement and discovery.

Swansea, Wales
February 2021

Acknowledgments

My thanks for many reasons to Areej Al-Kafaji, Alice Barale, David Jonathan Bayot, David Blakesley, Gary Day, Terry Eagleton, Torgeir Fjeld, Lisa Foran, Niall Gildea, Edward Greenwood, Rebekah Humphreys, Paddy Jemmer, Mike Jenkins, Peter Thabit Jones, Peter Lamarque, Rebecca Lowe, Marianna Papastephanou, Mike Quille, David and Emily Rothman, Martyn Sampson, Constantine Sandis, John Schad, Joe Sterrett, Jonathan Taylor, and Nithin Varghese. My wife Valerie was wonderfully patient, hugely supportive, and a great reader-out of my poems at various events, home and abroad. David Blakesley, my editor and publisher, did a wonderful job with *Socrates at Verse*, my previous Parlor Press book, and I am truly delighted to have this one appear under the same inspirational imprint.

I am also very grateful to the editors and publishers (often the same person) of *Culture Matters*, *Inscriptions*, *Scintilla*, *The Seventh Quarry*, *SubStance*, and *The Wednesday* for permission to reprint versions of poems that have appeared in their pages. Rahim and Wendy Hassan at *The Wednesday* have been especially generous with help, support and encouragement.

As Knowing Goes

For Valerie

We know so many things, as knowing goes.
We know each dawn will bring
A symphony of birdsong, why
They're tuning up to sing
A chant that grows
More clamorous as Spring
Returns, and why it fills the sky,
That restless carolling
Whose explanation every knower knows.

It's scientific lights we know them by,
These wonders we suppose
Must finally, like everything,
Be destined to disclose
What prompts that cry,
That keep-off call to foes,
Or mating-song, or tune to fling
Out wide and silence those
Loud conspecifics giving theirs a try.

Amongst things that elude such reckoning
Are bird-songs that defy,
Once heard, all bids to make plain prose
Of poetry, and shy
From honouring
Song-contracts that apply
Alike to nightingales and crows
Since framed to keep alerts set high
Lest songbirds too melodiously take wing.

We've slept through their awakening, and it shows.
That's why our senses cling
To broken scraps of song that tie

Us to the ding-a-ling
Of tweets and close
Our ears to the bright ring
Of a dawn-chorus primed to fly
Beyond the harkening
Of souls attuned to mundane ratios.

End-Time

> *The great majority of interpretations of Apocalypse assume that the End is pretty near. Consequently the historical allegory is always having to be revised; time discredits it. And this is important. Apocalypse can be disconfirmed without being discredited. This is part of its extraordinary resilience.*
>
> Frank Kermode, *The Sense of an Ending*

> *So when you see the desolating sacrilege spoken of by the prophet Daniel, standing in the holy place (let the reader understand), then let those who are in Judea flee to the mountain.*
>
> Matthew 24:15-16

They'd all troop up and then troop down again.
'Trust scripture, check the maths, end-times are nigh!'
Wrong call each time but now the truth stands plain.

Earthbound catastrophists alone stay sane
Since they're first off to raise the climate-cry,
Not just troop up and then troop down again.

Those old doom-sayers back up memory-lane
Devised new end-dates that would soon pass by:
Wrong call each time but now the truth stands plain.

'Another climb-down', the elect complain;
'Re-do the maths, give the I Ching a try.'
They all troop up and then troop down again.

Their loss of face brings joy to the profane
As dawn reveals no horsemen in the sky:
Wrong call each time but now the truth stands plain.

Through deft recalculations they maintain
The faith though unmet deadlines multiply:
They all troop up and then troop down again.

When drought, flood, forest-fire and hurricane
Spell doom for real, what need to prophesy?
Wrong call each time but now the truth stands plain.

They call down heavenly wrath yet call in vain:
It's we who've fixed the outcome, freeze or fry.
They'd all troop up and then troop down again,
Wrong call each time, but now the truth stands plain.

Odysseus at Forty

First you will come to the Sirens who enchant all who come near them. If any one unwarily draws in too close and hears the singing of the Sirens, his wife and children will never welcome him home again. . . . Therefore pass these Sirens by, and stop your men's ears with wax that none of them may hear; but if you like you can listen yourself, for you may get the men to bind you as you stand upright on a cross-piece half way up the mast, and they must lash the rope's ends to the mast itself, that you may have the pleasure of listening. If you beg and pray the men to unloose you, then they must bind you faster.

Homer, *The Odyssey*, Book XII, trans. Samuel Butler

Workers must look ahead with alert concentration and ignore anything which lies to one side. The urge toward distraction must be grimly sublimated in redoubled exertions. Thus the workers are made practical. The other possibility Odysseus chooses for himself, the landowner, who has others to work for him. He listens, but does so while bound helplessly to the mast . . . . Odysseus is represented in the sphere of work. Just as he cannot give way to the lure of self-abandonment, as owner he also forfeits participation in work and finally even control over it, while his companions, despite their closeness to things, cannot enjoy their work because it is performed under compulsion, in despair, with their senses forcibly stopped.

T.W. Adorno and Max Horkheimer, *Dialectic of Enlightenment*, trans. Edmund Jephcott

1

Why should those songs unheard now haunt my ear,
Disturb my nights, stir memories long subdued,
Count my great deeds a tedious traveller's tale,
And make this home, this Ithaca, a place
As strange to me as distant seas and skies?

No doubting Circe's words: 'Be sure to steer
Far wide of them, that sense-beguiling brood,
Those sirens whose allure, for those who sail
Too close to shore, will prove a foul embrace
Of evil masked in beauty's cunning guise.'

Thus her advice: 'if they, your sailors, hear
One note of it you'll soon find out you're crewed
By sex-drunk loons, so see to it that they'll
Have ears securely plugged lest such disgrace
Turn out your odyssey's enduring prize.'

Meanwhile I, as their leader, should appear
Strong-willed and resolute against those lewd
Yet lovely blandishments, so must not fail
To listen open-eared and yet, in case
Their spell prevails, make sure a shipmate ties

Me tight to the ship's mast. Then we'd not veer
From straight ahead despite the notes that wooed
My captive ear, notes sung to no avail
Since those unyielding ropes were there to brace
Me firm against all charms they might devise.

Master and crew: my task, to show that we're
'All in this thing together', though construed
More expertly it shows that there's a scale
That runs from those, like me, equipped to face
The threat head on and those whose ears or eyes

Need covering lest exposure cost us dear
As all succumb. And so it was we hewed
To a fixed course, ensured they not regale
Our sense with demon spells, and left that space
Of waking dream still echoing with their cries.

What if the crew repine? They know that we're
Born warriors and rulers while those rude
Mechanicals are there to row, to bail
Us out sometimes, or — on command — to chase
And sink the foe should proper cause arise.

For it was reason, vaunting yet austere,
That taught me those devices to preclude
The sirens' song, to fortify our frail
Sense-organs by the tricks on which I'd base
My game-plan when a fight-plan seemed unwise.

I think: one day they'll make it their idea,
Those future masters of the multitude
Who take my lead and play the alpha male,
While every gesture bears the ancient trace
Of women spurned to firm up social ties.

2

Yet there's another thought occurs to me
At times in this enforced retreat, this late
Retirement from the voyaging, the wars,
The monsters, the temptations, and the few
Brief times of joy such as — why now deny

The truth? — that mind-subduing melody
The sirens sang. Years on, I alternate
Between my stock account of it which draws
The usual moral and the one I drew
Back then while it was ringing still in my

Rapt ears and vibrant soul. Though Circe's plea
Determined me at first to navigate
As far from their sweet songs as from the jaws
Of Charybdis, I yet chose to pursue
That other, riskier course by which to try

What dreams, what visions, and what ecstasy
Might lie in store could we but contemplate
A realm beyond the future-binding laws
Of calculative reason. Why eschew
Such music at their chill command, and why

So readily accept the tale that she,
The sorceress Circe, opted to narrate,
Most likely with a view to settling scores
With some old deity or other who
Might help her out with Helios by and by

If I just played along. Penelope,
My poor long-suffering wife, had vowed to wait
In Ithaca and put her life on pause
Until my journey's end, so I should do
My best by her and let no vamp belie

My marriage-vows or count me devotee
Of her wild cult. Yet had I known my fate,
Years later, was to do the menial chores
And tend my crops and raise stout trees to hew
For strangers' ships then I'd have told them 'ply

An inshore course, unplug your ears, and be
My boon-companions in a change of state
Where beating hearts keep pace with beating oars
And warrior-captain shares with warrior-crew
The sound of souls attuned to sea and sky.'

You'll ask why the interpreters agree
With Circe, seeing fit to designate
That sorceress my advisor in the cause
Of *nostos*, truth and justice while they view
The sirens, with a prejudicial eye,

As demons any virtuous man would flee
Before their soul-corrupting poison bait
Could charm his ears. Yet who's to say it's whores
And temptresses alone whose songs subdue
Male reason or who scoff when men apply

Their repertoire of scheme and strategy
In ways that vainly strive to sublimate
All passion and desire? It's in the flaws
Of suchlike grand designs that they break through,
Those forces apt to send our plan awry

By giving voice to everything that we,
The planners, dread lest it initiate
Yet further sailings past yet further shores
Where wave-borne echoes shimmer in the blue
And souls re-echo to the sirens' cry.

Yet it's a sensual music, one set free
From soul's dominion and the body-hate
That comes of unchecked reason when it gnaws
At every bond of kind and kinship due
To fellow humans, be they low or high.

Take my Odyssean exploits as your key
To all life-passages and you'll negate
Whatever chance of happiness was yours
As each strategic game-plan steals from you
All hope of seizing pleasures as they fly.

My fate, to have the title 'Odyssey'
Forever linked to stories they'll relate,
Those bards, as if I merited applause
Solely for exploits hand-picked to accrue
Top marks from trickster, rogue, and clever-guy.

Some may remark the savage irony
Of this, a gist their tellings must dictate,
Not mine, since I've exhausted all my stores
Of irony along with derring-do,
Low cunning, guile, and meanings on the sly.

Think of me as a twice-born returnee,
The wily hero of an earlier date
Now turned a slave to memory who implores
No more than time enough to dream anew
Those voices Circe told me to defy.

Material: A Sonnet

> *There would be more kudos in allying myself with crystals—images of the seductive twinkling of snowflakes or diamonds—rather than grains which might conjure up no more exciting a picture than a handful of sand. Grains and crystals are rather like Cinderella before and after she goes to the ball.*
>
> Valerie Randle (Norris), 'The Cinderella of Sciencespeak'
>
> *This article surveys the current status of 'grain boundary engineering', i.e., the deliberate manipulation of grain boundary crystallography in polycrystals in order to produce a material containing grain boundaries which have superior properties compared to average boundaries.*
>
> Valerie Randle, abstract of article in *Acta Materialia*

Stress-tested and case-hardened, you and I,
Grain-boundaries aligned, good alloy steel.
See how tight-packed the latticed atoms lie!
Each flaw elucidates the pure ideal.
Your gift, to scan at microscopic scale,
Observe as streamed electrons find the flaws,
And then — in case some stressed component fail —
Review the crystallites, find out the cause.
Else bridges fall, jet aircraft crash and burn,
Space-rocket debris flames across the skies
As seals corrode, and lovers fail to learn
From those, like you, keen-eyed and boundary-wise.
No alloy, no soul-union, where no plea
On matter's part for mind's microscopy.

Ancrene Wisse*

Life as an anchoress began with a death. On entering their cell for the first time, the novice recluse would climb into a grave dug inside the cell. . . . Some directions state that [they] should pause at the opening of the cell and the bishop should say 'Si vult intrare, intret' ('if she wishes to go in, allow her to go in'). . . . The anchoress would then climb into the grave, where she was sprinkled with earth—ashes to ashes, dust to dust—and the door of the cell was bolted.

Mary Wellesley, 'Thys Place is Pryson', *London Review of Books*, 23rd May 2019, p. 3.

1

He visits, I await with lowered veil
His Grace the Bishop in my tiny cell,
Not meeting yet envisioning his gaze
Fixed hard upon me as we join in prayer.

'Your spirit's strong', he says, 'but flesh is frail;
Be not so reticent, I wish you well,
As witness this my hand that gently lays
Its blessing on these earthly pains you bear.'

Yes, pains enough, but none to match his tale
Of how the punishments laid up in hell
Would, by God's grace, diminish as each day's
Self-chastisement increased my heaven-share.

See where our clutching hands have worn the rail
Down thin with prayer, all we who chose to dwell,
Singly and unto death, where no light plays
Save lurid shapes cast by a candle's flare.

---

* *Ancrene Wisse* (*Guide for Anchoresses*) is an early thirteenth-century text, almost certainly written by a man, which lays down rules and received practices for female anchorites. These were women—like the best-known of them, Dame Julian of Norwich—who consented to seclude themselves under physical conditions of extreme hardship in pursuit of spiritual purity and wisdom.

Yet it's not these privations most assail
My spirit, nor the soul-subduing knell
That sounds each time the passing bell conveys
Its gist: 'Dead to the world; now who's to care?.'

Much more it's how he visits without fail,
The Bishop, when there comes another spell
Of unsought ecstasy that bids me raise
My eyes, then see him waiting, watching there.

He speaks of demon armies set to scale
My earthen walls, of senses that rebel
In Satan's cause, and all the thousand ways
Their soul-assaults may tempt me to despair.

Two visitants there are who haunt my gaol,
Bishop and Satan, or — I cannot tell —
Just one, his double aspect donned to craze
My mind and yield me up to Satan's snare.

At times I think: how should he not prevail,
The silk-robed fiend whose overtures repel
Yet mesmerise this captive soul who prays
That faith tell them apart, that kindred pair.

Else why the torments laid on tooth and nail,
The scourges, self-inflictions, infidel
Thought-whispers, or his blessing that betrays
Us both to every devil we'd foreswear.

2

Her visage showed distinctly through the gauze,
The veil put on to cast off worldly ties,
As I performed the rituals of retreat
And cursed each monstrous word I had to say.

Perhaps I glimpsed some momentary pause,
Some drawing back, some movement of the eyes,
As if she thought: for one last time let's cheat
This living death, this grotesque passion-play!

Yet her sworn contract held no exit-clause,
No get-out that would have us recognise
(Dear God!) warm flesh beneath the winding-sheet
Or life unlived as not her debt to pay!

Time was I felt it too, that fire that draws
Fresh anchorites like her to improvise
New modes of suffering, new ways to beat
Off Satan's lure or end the Devil's sway.

Yet how describe the Moloch-God who gnaws
At their young hearts, these women who chastise
Themselves as an inquisitor might treat
Heresiarchs who lead poor souls astray.

O watch in horror as she kicks and claws
Loose earth about the burrow where she lies,
As if to stage her sepulture and meet
Death running in her funeral array.

A fine performance, worthy the applause
Of those old ghouls who'd come to solemnize
This deathly tryst as if she were some peat-
Bog sacrificial victim on display.

They use you like so many virgin-whores
Or bringers-on of lust in pious guise
And count it virtuous, though no less sweet,
The dream-sin shared as saint and sinner pray.

Such torment when the sacristan then pours
His box of dust and bids her now arise
And quit the scene, else lay those hands and feet
Where faith alone can keep despair at bay.

A score of lives I've brought to this, but yours
The conscience-racking memory that defies
All hope of some blest afterlife to greet
My soul while yours frets out its mortal way.

Negentropes: Two Poems

We may express in the following manner the fundamental laws of the universe which correspond to the two fundamental theorems of the mechanical theory of heat: the energy of the universe is constant; the entropy of the universe tends to a maximum.

    Rudolf Clausius, *The Mechanical Theory of Heat*

When things don't change any longer, that's the end result of entropy, the heat-death of the universe. The more things go on moving, interrelating, conflicting, changing, the less balance there is—and the more life.

    Ursula K. LeGuin, *The Lathe of Heaven*

How would we express in terms of the statistical theory the marvellous faculty of a living organism, by which it delays the decay into thermodynamical equilibrium (death)? . . . . The device by which an organism maintains itself stationary at a fairly high level of orderliness . . . really consists in continually sucking orderliness from its environment.

    Erwin Schrödinger, *What Is Life?*

1

Heat-death resets all metrics back to nil.
It's what doom-tellers sync their watches by.
No scale to reckon on once time stands still.

Count climate-change no halt to the big chill
Though forests burn and fire-storms light the sky:
Heat-death resets all metrics back to nil.

Micro or macro, all states run downhill
To zero absolute where they supply
No scale to reckon on once time stands still.

Take long views and the end-state must fulfil
That second law, the one that tells us why
Heat-death resets all metrics back to nil.

Entropy, like the world-tree Yggdrasil,
Keeps all in order till all orders die:
No scale to reckon on once time stands still.

We rate our chances life-wise, freeze or grill,
Though physics-wise the odds stack extra-high:
Heat-death resets all metrics back to nil.

Run mortal life-grist through the physics-mill
And fluctuant void is all you'll quantify:
No scale to reckon on once time stands still.

Yet maybe it's our physics-nurtured drill,
That leap to how the laws of science lie:
'Heat-death resets all metrics back to nil.'

Think Pascal's twin sublime, his terror-thrill
As thought goes infinite in the mind's eye.
No scale to reckon on once time stands still;
Heat-death resets all metrics back to nil.

2

It's living things alone that slow the rate.
Negentropy's what keeps the chill at bay.
How else delay that zero-action state,
That cosmic analogue of groundhog-day?

Left to themselves, all states equilibrate,
Run down at last, hit the entropic hay;
Why then think life exempt from that dark fate
Decreed for atoms as for mortal clay?

What's life? asked Schrödinger, and took the trait
In question as the role that life-forms play
In making room for physics to create
New order from entropic disarray.

No putting off our short expiry-date,
Us and those fellow creatures sadly prey
To death, disease and what our genes dictate
As unwished endings to our earthly stay.

That's not his point, the fact that they equate
As co-extensive, 'life' and 'death-delay',
Nor that some stronger life-force might negate
And block the threats now barrelling our way.

More it's that we'll do better, as we wait
For signs of doom, if minded to defray
The psychic toll with thoughts that compensate
By having long perspectives to convey.

Then, though the climate warnings come too late
And all things fleshly track their own decay,
Still we've sufficient grounds to celebrate
What Schrödinger had grounds enough to say.

For who needs Maxwell's Demon at the gate,
That impish fixer-up of how things lay
By tweaking molecules to indicate
One case where entropy renounced its sway?

A thought-trick merely, but why cultivate
Absurd hypotheses when, come what may,
We've music, books, ideas, and the whole slate
Of arts and sciences that bid us pay

Due heed to how life's energies checkmate
The second law, how mutant DNA
Wrests order from disorder, and how great
The gap its a-life replicants betray.

Endolphins

> *'Yeah', said David. 'We could just do bicycle. Anything to get the endorphins going.'*
>
> *Ryan lay flat-out on the sofa and had covered himself with cushions.*
>
> *'Dorphins. Isn't that what dolphins have?'*
>
> *'Endorphins are what make you feel nice', said David.*
>
> Aiden Shaw, *Wasted*

They ask 'How so lively, so active and fit,
You old guy with your three-score and ten,
Always off to the gym in your exercise kit
To work out with those sporty young men?.'
I just tell them straight out, 'It's the dolphins, that's it;
They got me up and running again.'

Then they ask 'What's your secret, what keeps you awake
When you're staying out late on the tiles,
When you've danced till the small hours with scarcely a break
And it's time to walk home all those miles?.'
Then I say 'It's them dolphins, they'll be there to make
A night-picnic of life's little trials.'

Or they say 'Don't you think it's high time you acquired
A demeanour more suiting your age?
Just admit it: the wild nights are leaving you tired,
Let the stop-out give way to the sage!.'
But I say 'It's them dolphins who keep me all fired-
Up and fit for my nightly rampage.'

Then they tell me the dolphins will do me no good
When I'm fighting for breath in the gym,
And the guys are all saying 'Poor bloke, but he would
Push himself — no more dolphins for him!.'
Yet their frolics revive me as nothing else could
When my dolphins get back in the swim.

For a life without dolphins is no life at all,
Not a life for high-fliers like me,
Since it's dolphins alone keep your eye on the ball
And your body-mass low as can be.
O it's dolphins that leap in me, dolphins whose call
Fills my soul like the call of the sea.

Then they tell me 'The dolphins are making you look
Very foolish — please give them a rest,
Take a leaf out of our grow-old-gracefully book,
And give up on your juvenile quest.'
But I say 'It's them dolphins got me off the hook
And then jacked up my personal best.'

So I'll cherish the dolphins as they speed their way
To my brain on that mind-blowing trip,
While I cheer them along and attempt to repay
All their gifts to me when I let rip,
Till I frolic no more though the dolphins still play
In the wake of my shaky old ship.

An Eton Mess

We're in an Eton mess, my friends,
We're in an Eton mess.
Those posh-boy crooks have cocked their snooks
And cooked the books when no one looks:
That's how it goes I guess, my friends,
That's how it goes I guess.

We're back up Eton creek, my mates,
We're back up Eton creek.
Those stuck-up fools from public schools
Have bribed their tools and fixed the rules
To suit their crony clique, my mates,
To suit their crony clique.

They lied to win our votes, you folk,
They lied to win our votes.
They said 'Vote leave, one final heave',
But whispered 'We've tricks up our sleeve',
And now they're at our throats, you folk,
And now they're at our throats.

They played the racist card, old chums,
They played the racist card.
They said 'we'll claw back cash galore
If we show more of them the door.'
They hit the migrants hard, old chums,
They hit the migrants hard.

It's you they're out to screw, you lot,
It's you they're out to screw.
They say the gains outweigh the pains
But use your brains, you're still in chains:
You'll starve before they're through, you lot,
You'll starve before they're through.

Fight back and see them off at last!
Fight back and see them off.
Just seize the day, make that lot pay,
Get back what they have stashed away
And stuff that tosspot toff at last,
And stuff that tosspot toff.

You'll clear the Eton mess all right,
You'll clear the Eton mess.
You'll hold the pass, put ruling-class
Dolts out to grass, and kick some ass:
One gang of thieves the less all right,
One gang of thieves the less.

Rank-Shifting: An Allegory[*]

I reign high castled in my seigneur state,
They service me, I lord it mightily,
Yet still she's moated and inviolate,
This upstart wench who wall-walks over me.

Her virtue's motte-and-baileyed from attack,
My siege repulsed, portcullissed, put to flight
While she, fine-finialled, finds out every crack
And sappers these my walls in love's despite.

How rampart my defences when desire
Runs riot through my gates unsentinelled
And press-gangs the unruly troop whose hire
Now leaves me sally-ported, self-repelled.

I courtly-love her but she'll curtly shove
My pleas aside, fast-bar the oubliette
For my deep bolting-down, and up above
Sport wanton with that pilfer-pantry set.

Speech-parts refunctioned mark old chaos come
Again, love's code dechivalried, the rules
Of grammar wild, uncastellanned, and some
Lord-Anarch loosed in all the language-schools.

Behold me now, versed in the courtly art
Of body-parts decoupled that decrees
My coat-of-arms a high-embrasured heart
That unschooled soldiery can pierce with ease.

---

[*] 'Rank-shifting' is a technical term in systemic linguistics which I've used, in a non-technical (inaccurate) way, to indicate departures from normal usage with regard to grammatical or part-of-speech categories like noun, verb, adjective, and adverb. It is a frequent feature of some poetry such as that of Shakespeare, Gerard Manley Hopkins and Dylan Thomas. In this poem rank-shifting also has to do with castles, courtly love, and subversions of authority and power.

It's by rank-shifting that the low upend
The high, that lordship's scullioned, and that my
Fierce heart lies dungeoned till it deigns to bend
Its knee to her, now chatelained on high.

I'm postern-gated, castle-keep-confined,
My bridge undrawn, my soul lèse-majesté'd
As she disintricates the ties that bind
The sluice and foes upswarm the escalade.

Another Journey*

The historical sense compels a man to write not merely with his own generation in his bones, but with a feeling that the whole of the literature of Europe from Homer and within it the whole of the literature of his own country has a simultaneous existence and composes a simultaneous order.

T.S. Eliot, 'Tradition and the Individual Talent' (1919)

The population should be homogeneous; where two or more cultures exist in the same place they are likely either to be fiercely self-conscious or both to become adulterate. What is still more important is unity of religious background; and reasons of race and religion combine to make any large number of free-thinking Jews undesirable.

T.S. Eliot, *After Strange Gods: A Primer of Modern Heresy* (1934)

We ought not to seek to outlaw Eliot's poems, but neither can we submit to them. We should not ban them; but we must not abandon ourselves to them. Instead we must contest that poetry, with strategies that acknowledge both its value and its menace.

Anthony Julius, *The Guardian* 7th June 2003

---

* This verse-essay takes the form of a dramatic monologue imagined as spoken by a political refugee from a country torn by civil strife since its deliverance from British colonial rule. His reflections range over history, politics, his family's sufferings during their enforced flight, and their far from welcoming reception on arriving in Britain. He also talks about his highly ambivalent—or drastically polarized—attitude to British culture, especially the university education in English Literature and cultural theory that the speaker has received and that fills him, now, with a mixture of pride, guilt, disdain, and a resolve to turn it back against his teachers and literary mentors. Most prominent of them is T.S. Eliot who stands for everything he finds most politically repulsive in that culture along with everything most subtly alluring. Eliot's popular 'Journey of the Magi' comes in here as a prominent intertext and a source of numerous ironic contrasts with the speaker's current situation. The poem is written in 'free verse' mode—actually a basic four-beat line with free-ish variations—so as to convey something of the Eliotic verse-music along with its frequent undecidable mixture of modest, mock-modest, persuasive, manipulative, and downright coercive rhetoric.

> *. . . the cities hostile and the towns unfriendly*
> *And the villages dirty and charging high prices:*
> *A hard time we had of it.*
> *At the end we preferred to travel all night,*
> *Sleeping in snatches,*
> *With voices singing in our ears, saying*
> *That this was all folly.*
>
>   T.S. Eliot, 'Journey of the Magi'

The hardest of hard journeys we had of it,
The lands we passed through hostile and menacing,
The seas mostly rough, always unpredictable,
The people-traffickers abusive, rapacious,
And at every border the humiliating questions,
The routine threat, whether voiced or unspoken,
Of being sent 'home' to the place we'd come from,
And facing again the necessity of explaining
To our frightened, hungry and exhausted children
Why we were treated as strangers and parasites,
Deserving at best their administered charity,
At worst their unconcealed hatred and contempt,
Whipped up every day by the tabloid press,
By politicians in quest of the populist vote,
Or by those who unthinkingly do their work
In the social media where any non-belonger
To some online 'community' is, for that reason,
An intruder, a threat, an unwanted alien,
Or 'potential terrorist', as the weasel-phrase goes,
Like 'potential enemy' or 'potential rapist',
Those slippery locutions that serve so well
In their role as spreaders of hatred and suspicion
Toward us folk thrown on your state's tender mercies.

My friends, I ask you only: please try to imagine
How it was for us, once we actually got here,
Once we somehow managed to cross the last obstacle,
Your narrow, almost risk-free English Channel
To this place of deliverance from all our afflictions,

The reward for all our dangers and hardships en route,
The land where our kids might size us up again,
Perhaps even think: 'Ah, they're human after all,
Decent people with a claim to shared humanity
And not, as we had almost come to conclude,
The authors of some unknown outrage against it,
Condemning us forever to our stateless wandering
In the purlieus of suspicion and the bad precincts
Where often it seemed that the one thing we shared,
Us migrants, was the fact of our non-belonging,
The fragile, self-protective solidarity that comes
When everyone within striking or snooping range
Most likely has some score to settle with you.

So: at evening we came (I continue my allusion
To your poet T.S. Eliot's 'Journey of the Magi',
Although, truth to tell, I am less than enamored
Of its Anglican piety, its labored symbolism,
And the long history of prejudice and violence
Concealed by its suave deportment and cadences) —
We came, I say, to a land of indifferent weather,
Of unremarkable landscapes, its people not given
To much in the way of strong or unruly passions,
And with a history no doubt rich in incident
To their mostly placid, insular way of thinking,
But one that seemed to us quite pitifully lacking
In the epic dimension, the scenes of high drama,
The treacherous depths, the savage complexities,
And, to cite once more that Virgilian polisher
Of phrases, the 'cunningly contrived corridors'
That have made of our own, more recent history
A nightmare one escapes from only at the cost
Of a deeply felt — call it spiritual — deprivation,
One unknown to you surely heaven-blest dwellers
In a united kingdom, or united enough
At least to save it from the alternating miseries
Of civil war, exodus, or just being constantly
At one another's throats.

        You might have called it satisfactory
Had that first state of things improved even slightly,
Had our landing on these shores after such a journey
Been greeted, not perhaps with heartfelt joy
Or displays of sympathy on a grandiose scale,
But in the knowledge that we had, after all,
Arrived by the longest, most arduous of routes
From hell on earth to a place where the natives
(Forgive my usage) had reason to be thankful
For having so far witnessed nothing to compare
With such extremes of physical or mental pain,
And might thus be expected, in natural justice,
To grant us the right of domicile in their country,
Along with some adequate means of subsistence,
Respect for our culture, schooling for our children,
And acceptance — though we don't push it too hard,
You'll understand — that it was their governments
Who'd joined with our home-grown tyrants to spawn
The post-colonial horrors that drove us into exile,
A piecemeal diaspora that has gone unrecorded
In the annals or the gospels of those exiled peoples
More PR-minded than us, or just better placed
To work up their suffering into a providential tale
And turn it back on conqueror and victim alike.

We arrived two years ago though it feels a lifetime,
And still I'm here with my wife, children and a few
Familiar compound ghosts in a 'short-term' holding camp
Where the guards or warders (how else describe them?)
Do their utmost to strip us of every last dignity,
Every shred of self-respect that we'd somehow held onto,
And where our kids ask again: what parents are these
Who have brought us to this drab suburb of Purgatory,
Fed us stories of a land where the insults and terrors
Would at last be made up for by acts of kindness,
Yet delivered us into the hands of new enemies
Who differ from the old ones solely in so far
As their cruelty has a more briskly bureaucratic,

Less overtly threatening but just as effective
Range of methods for crushing any life-hopes retained
Through all the dismal stations of our journey to date.

'But this set down', your poet has his magus say,
And again, 'this set down', with that trademark air
Of scriptural *gravitas* that masks its purpose
Behind a narrative and a language expertly honed
Over the centuries by those whose task it was,
Or whose 'vocation' when suitably kitted out
In theological garb, to place the formal seal
Of church-and-state approval on such fine tales
As tell of star-led journeys, celestial portents,
And travellers, like the sadder-but-wiser Magi,
Returning unmolested to their distant palaces
And sherbet-girls. Meanwhile, unknown to them,
Herod's soldiers go on with the requisite slaughter
Of infants by the thousand, and history goes on
With its routine business, in Auden's less unctuous
Though scarcely more kindly or comfortable words,
Of refusing to help or to pardon those earmarked
As simply 'the defeated' while none the less adding,
Albeit *sotto voce* or strictly off the record,
Its mealy-mouthed 'alas!' in token recognition
That the star-roles have long since gone to the villains,
The conquerors, or the late-triumphing victims,
Those bouncers-back whom history afterwards showed
To have been, so to speak, on the right wrong side
Of the victory-parade, unlike us who keep clutching
Our alien gods.

    I trust you'll not have concluded
That I, a lifelong reader and devoted student
Of English Literature, a graduate in that discipline,
And a product of your own truly splendid system
For its conveyance to colonials and post-colonials —
Not concluded, I say, that it's one more instance
Of that overworked trope, 'The Empire Writes Back',

Even if I've given voice to a certain special animus
Against Archbishop Eliot as, of all modern poets,
He who did most to set the tone and the syllabus,
'Literary' as well as cultural-historical-political,
For coaxing generations of complicitous readers
To accept that ultra-civilized yet lethal concoction
Of snobbery, religiosity, thinly-veiled racism,
And — as even his greatest admirers acknowledge,
If they've the keenness of ear to perceive it —
The extent and depth of those Eliotic prejudices
To be heard in so many long-familiar passages,
In the phrasing, verse-rhythms, and frequent tone
Of mock-diffident assurance, or self-irony mixed
With the kind of presumptive authority that comes
So naturally of writing, as he schooled us to believe,
With all the history of Christian and Classical Europe
'In one's bones', along with the placid awareness
(Not unknown among your Home Office officials)
Of embodying the interests and values of a clerisy
To whose sole keeping is entrusted the knowledge
Of what constitutes *culture* as distinct from *cultures*,
Or merits the attention of literary critics,
Not the Gurkha regiments of Cultural Studies.

Please forgive, then, this brash and vulgar intrusion
By one of your culture's (I confess) disenchanted
Yet not altogether unappreciative products
When he seeks, with a return to that 'sly civility'
Much theorized by the Cultural Studies people
As their subaltern rejoinder to the Lit Crit guys —
When he seeks, as I do, to regain your attention
And suggest, speaking very much as 'one of yours',
That the barbarians are already inside your gates,
Though not in the guise of your criminals, deviants,
Street-people, unemployed, benefit claimants,
'Skivers' as opposed to 'strivers', gender misfits,
Or indeed — to assume my own designated place
In this tabloid litany — refugees, asylum-seekers,

'Economic migrants', and those who arrive
Seeking long-term redress for the manifold crimes
Committed against them not only by the masters,
But also by the dedicated culture-servants
Ever busied about their masters' business.

Consider, if you will, the scholar-literati
Of an empire whose reach, in its time near-global,
Narrows now to the point of a stylistic inflection,
A judicious turn of phrase, a well-placed comma,
A subtly nuanced view of literary history,
Or a deployment of just those scriptural tonings
Reliably conducive to just what's required
In the way of response, both from those well-trained
To come running at such high-cultural whistles,
And also — alas — from those whose every conscious,
Every critically aware or reflective inclination
Is to take that still potent ideology apart,
And do so using all the fine devices picked up
Through a lengthy education, suffered or enjoyed,
At the hands of their masters, mentors and poets.

Let me not, for all that, become too much addicted
To the ever seductive since ever-so-human
Role of victim-accuser, a role better suited
To those who've lost out in every possible way,
Whose lives have touched the absolute degree zero
Of what lives should be if they're to count as 'human',
Since — unlike me, as you'll probably be thinking —
They don't have 'the education it takes' to get quits
With both the old rulers and their dissident heirs,
Those post-colonial theorists who craftily rework
All the tropes and tricks devised during a half-century
Of table-turning techniques and refinements.

I write these thoughts — these ideas you'll recognize
As trained up in just such post-colonialist ways —
Because they're ideas that 'come naturally' to me,

Or rather because it is so hard to tell what's natural
From what's 'second nature', the latter then taken
(Unless you're a devotee of the tabloid papers)
As signaling some large and unwitting contribution
From the idioms of 'common sense', popular belief,
Or (excuse the intrusion of such vulgar jargon)
Right-wing ideology. I write them because, plainly,
They are thoughts of the kind I was taught to think
By tutors and critics who had nothing in common
With your immigration officers, court officials,
Benefits assessors, Home Secretaries, and so forth,
Except — as with Eliot's strangely popular poem
And its certified exegetes — the apostolic tone
Of perfect self-assurance and presumed right to judge
In the name of all thinking, cultivated persons,
Or as God's (their own God's) authorized deputies
On an earth still cross-hatched, in their mental maps,
By borders that follow no topographic contours
But solely the edicts of government committees,
Advisory bodies, and 'expert informants'
Or scholars who just chanced to fetch up 'in the field.'

After such knowledge, as he says, what forgiveness?
What forgiveness for me who have broken the rules
Of civilized taste, not to mention academic discourse?
What forgiveness for you (if in 'you' I am permitted
To conflate the mixed company of everyone named
In this rambling tirade) who have, in your no doubt
Very different ways, firmed up the contingencies
Of your short-lived imperium and decreed them signs
Of a non-contingent since historically predestined
Or sacrosanct order? What forgiveness, again,
For my exploiting here the most advanced ideas
Of your ultra-refined literary scholarship
In order to launch another Oedipal assault
On all that went to construct them? And permit me
One last bitter twist of the knife: what forgiveness
For one who indulges these self-shriving thoughts,

These interminable probings of critical conscience,
When faced, he and his family, with the evidence
On your streets, in your tabloids, and in the chatter
Of your leading politicians or opinion-formers
That time is very short and that theory, in the end,
Has rather little to say on more urgent topics,
Such as how to talk honestly to your children,
How persuade them that attending a British school
Is something they'll not at all regret having done
Even if, needless to say, they hate having to do it,
Or again, how explain that, despite all I've said,
An education by these, their teachers in a new life,
Is a tainted chalice that's well worth the taking
And payback, in some sort, for the old oppressors.

For once inside their citadel you acquire this knack
Of getting inside the heads, the thoughts and feelings
Of the cleverest mind-benders, Eliot among them,
Who have fashioned the very terms of our victimage
Through a cultural discourse that played its own role,
Discreet though effective, in their mission to ensure
That nothing should disturb the predestined order
Of languages, cultures, and well-regulated lives
Whose record is inscribed, as Walter Benjamin said,
On every monument of civilization and barbarism,
On your poet's finely-pitched tonal intimations,
And on his thoughts concerning the undesirability
Of 'free-thinking Jews' beyond a certain fixed quota
Finding house-room in 'our' cultural midst, or again,
In his lines about the 'hooded hordes swarming
Over endless plains', their location vague and distant
The more forcefully to vouch their savage alterity,
Yet not so far off as to lessen their imminent threat
To 'our' classically-divinely ordained way of life.

I admit: there were brain-worm thoughts, phrases
And images of yours that once I shored against my ruin,
Maybe thinking that a dose of the master's medicine,

If administered with sufficient grace of utterance,
Might lend an equivalent weight and authority
To our own, albeit more astutely critical
Since dissident ways of thought, while drawing notice
To our special kind of inwardness with a culture
That required we exhibit such renegade allegiance
If our writings were not to be dismissed as products
Of a culturally alien, a distorted since 'provincial'
Grasp of the finer points. Call it collaboration,
If you like, or sleeping with the enemy, or maybe
Something worse, but do give us credit at least,
Us reverse Calibans, for deploying that knowledge
To turn insults back and so, by sheer civility,
Stick inky fingers up to your own native Calibans,
Your fools-in-office, your dimwit politicians,
And your cabinet ministers to whom Oxford
Is a fast-track finishing school for wealthy idiots,
Those upon whose brutish nature, as Prospero says,
'Nurture cannot stick.'

    If the empire writes back
Then it will be by learning from your best and worst,
Or those who mix best and worst in themselves, like Eliot,
The meme-artificers and spinners of a haunting line
In poetry or prose that often chimes softly
With barbarous themes — like Eliot's refined *Kulturkampf*
Or Prospero's spell-bound regime — and yet gives a hold
For us cuckoos, pitch-perfect colonists of your nest,
To ventriloquize our grievances in a subaltern key
And in some part redeem our obeisance to the masters
By rendering our tributes of skewed intent, our homage
Of tweaked meanings, or our revisionary ratios,
Adopted as often from those writers most complicit
In our histories of exile, humiliation and despair
As from those, the devisers of our fight-back strategy,
Whose texts bear all the obdurate witness-marks
Of that same old inner strife.

Think of me, should you wish,
As a riled-up avatar of Arnold's scholar-gypsy,
Though one whose journey has been forced upon him
By factors beyond his grasp, let alone control,
And who has here done his best, in however confused
Or piecemeal a fashion, to contrive some narrative
That would fit them all in, all the crazily ill-matched
Parts of a life that found so much of its meaning
In the ideas, speech-rhythms, niceties, nuances,
And Eliot-inflected gestures of assurance
That somehow survived every border-guard-inflicted
Reminder of how little such attainments count for
In one whose situation declares them invalid,
Or serves as yet another standing provocation
To the guardians of native, homegrown English culture
Against the now civilized, well-schooled barbarians.

On Dover Quay I can connect/Nothing with nothing.
You taught me literature, and my profit on't/
Is I know to curse. Who are these hordes swarming
Across walls and borders, stumbling over questions,
Ringed by the bureaucracies of a dozen alien kingdoms?
We shall not cease from forced migration,
And the end of all our years-long futile wandering
Is to arrive at a hostile place like where we started
And know it for the third, fifth, twentieth time.
In our godforsaken end is our godforsaken beginning.
I voice his words, much of the time, and go . . .
Who is the second self who walks always beside you?
You must go by the way of dispossession.
Moi! Hypocrite lecteur,—son semblable,—son frère!

Diamantine: an exchange

> *Lab-grown diamonds have the same chemical and physical properties as naturally mined diamonds, with even industry experts unable to tell the difference optically.*
>
> *'One was manufactured in a laboratory and one was formed in the earth over billions of years, so there is a significant difference in value', says Cathleen McCarthy, founder of the Jewellery Loupe blog. 'I would hope the public sees that difference, because it should be reflected in the price they pay.'*
>
> *'I just want to give people choice. You want to marry a gerbil? Marry a gerbil. God bless', says Weindling. 'I wasn't here to judge other people, but I can judge myself very harshly. I won't touch a mined diamond. I have one left, it's the one I gave my wife 20 years ago. It's for sale. If you want to buy it, just make me an offer.'*
>
> Oliver Milman, 'Are Laboratory-Grown
Diamonds the More Ethical Choice to Say "I
Do"?', *The Guardian*, March 10th, 2020

A

A diamond ring, stone perfect, solitaire,
Earth-nurtured, no mere artefact, not made
To order in some lab set up to do
The work of ages quickly, day by day.

They sell it short, the jewellers, when they dare
Profane such mysteries by some parade
Of flashy stuff, or saying 'they'll accrue
More wealth, those items in the real-stone tray.'

For it's beyond all thought of market-share
Or value-added worth, the homage paid
By mortal souls to what shines forth anew
At each day's dawn, redeems the old cliché

'Love reigns supreme', has wonders to declare
Amongst the pile of tawdrier goods displayed
In late-life retrospect, and lets us two
Count all eternity our time to pay.

I say: your ersatz diamond's fashion-wear,
A glitzy substitute whose charms will fade
When set against the undeceiving hue
Of stones sky-lit by every tangent ray.

B

The science says: no difference, go compare!
You think one's 'real', the other sort low-grade
Since lab-produced, but take the close-up view
And which is which? Microscopy won't say.

You think the 'genuine' specimens are rare,
Like loving hearts and marriages, since laid
Down deep where processes run slow but true
And scales are reckoned on the *longue durée*.

Nice thought alright, though you'd much better spare
Another one for those to whom the trade
In 'genuine' diamonds brought a witches' brew
Of suffering, death and slavery their way.

No doubt you'll say: the artefacts have their
Environmental cost when duly weighed
In terms of all the oomph it takes to screw
The pressures up, ensure state-changes stay

On target, have the ecosystem bear
Whatever strain this causes, and evade
The charge that otherwise would finger you
Hephaestus-types as time-lords fit to slay!

But that's a message that should rightly scare
Both parties to this 'natural'/'fake' charade
Since, mined or lab-grown, diamonds always skew
Dame Nature's course and send our wits astray.

A

You'll say they conjure castles in the air,
Mere fantasies of ours, like lumps of jade
Taken for emeralds, those stones we blew
Small fortunes on for bride or fiancée,

As if she really cared — or ought to care —
When force of custom managed to persuade
Her doting mate to stump it up on cue,
That price deemed fitting for a life-time lay!

You'll ask: why ape the spendthrift millionaire?
They've small intrinsic worth, so why be swayed
By fetishized commodities and coo
When they invite to glitter and be gay?

But if the answer to a lover's prayer
For constancy and truth is best conveyed
By natural stones, not those we take in lieu,
Then it's in virtue of the role they play

In gift-relations such that we foreswear
All thought of recompense, of gems arrayed
Like IOUs, and pay the tribute due
To all that long outlasts our mortal clay,

That 'makes one little room an everywhere',
Holds fast through vows forgotten or betrayed,
Transcends the antics of the human zoo,
And yields a scent *absente de tous bouquets*.

B

You old romantics with your famous flair
For that 'moth-eaten musical brocade'
Of symbol, myth, and all the ballyhoo
It takes to keep reality at bay!

This much I'll grant: not really our affair,
Us physics buffs, but there's that 'golden braid'
The others speak of, those who find a clue
To such arcana in the stuff that they

Know lots about like logic, maths and (snare
Of diamond-fanciers!) how Ockham's blade
Still needs to do its job of cutting through
The verbiage spawned by folk-naïveté.

For maybe — maybe! — it's the case that they're
Not fools but onto something, that brigade
Of would-be alchemists keen to imbue
Their stones with properties so *recherché*.

Perhaps — perhaps! — they're simply out to square
That glimpsed eternity with all that they'd
So long self-willed to credit yet half-knew
Must shun the scientific light of day.

A

Could be there's cause for glory and despair
In those, like us, entranced yet half-afraid,
When index of refraction shows up blue,
That, truth to tell, the real's all grey-on-grey.

Let's say: what holds us spellbound in the *clair-
Obscur* of diamantine light and shade
May beckon when you physicists pursue
Your passion, dazzle or darken as it may.

After Lockdown

No we'll not go back to the bad old days,
To the days of graft and greed,
When the wealthy went their crooked ways,
And the worker went in need.
For when viruses strike it's the poor guy pays,
The guy with mouths to feed,
As the thing goes into its critical phase
And the reaper gets up to speed.

Oh we'll not go back to the years we spent
Being told how things were fine,
Though the good things went to the 1%
And the crap to the 99,
While they tried to stifle the discontent
Among those way back in line
By treating the Coronavirus 'event'
As a test of our moral spine!

But we'll not go back to their crafty tales,
To their trickery, scams and lies,
To the nincompoops raised as alpha-males,
And the hedge-fund hiking guys.
For their plan's a sure winner, it works if it fails:
They just go for the rip-off prize
Till it all goes wrong and a long spell in gaol's
The just sentence that never applies.

For we'll not go back to that time before
The Coronavirus struck,
Though it struck the harder if you were poor,
Or disabled, or down on your luck,
And not raking it in like those devil's spore
Out to screw you and make a fast buck
From the plagues of the time, whether sickness or war,
With us lot as their sitting duck.

No we'll not go back to all that again,
To the age of executive jets,
When the wealthy could always hop on a plane
And then life would be good as it gets.
For it's clear as day if you've half a brain
That their grounding's no cause for regrets,
Now the skies show blue through the window-pane
And the Sun gleams bright as it sets.

No, we'll not go back to the days of old
When racketeers ran the show,
When we swallowed those lies the fat cats sold
And the rip-offs they had on the go,
While their tame politicians did all they were told,
Cashed in on the quid pro quo,
And the huddling masses, left out in the cold,
Were the last who got to know.

Yes, those were the dog days we had to get through,
Like when Covid 19 hit its peak,
When the doctors and nurses did all they could do
But a vaccine was still far to seek,
And we suddenly knew, as the death-figures grew,
That for us lot the prospects were bleak
Since we all, nervous sailors and medical crew,
Were headed up Corona Creek.

But know this: if there's one bit of wisdom we learned,
As we fretted lest months become years,
It's that even the worst of events can be turned
To good purpose as retrospect clears.
For there's strength to be had from those lessons hard-earned,
From the hopes intermixed with the fears,
And the new life discerned as we lock-downers yearned
To make good on our lives in arrears.

So there's no going back to how matters stood then,
No regressing to times gone by,

When the captains of commerce were masters of men
And their whims could decide: live or die!
Yes, we lived through the virus and told ourselves: when
This thing's finished we'll want to know why
The old fixers and fraudsters had done it again,
Screwed us over and wrung us out dry.

Now we've made good and sure their devices won't come
Back and bite us like last time around,
That the money-men won't get us under their thumb
Till we end up six feet underground,
That their mansion won't tower over our urban slum
Where the viral infections abound,
And that never again shall they do zero-sum
Calculation of lives to the pound.

Tampering

Out of the quarrel with others we make rhetoric; out of the quarrel with ourselves we make poetry.

        W.B. Yeats

For poetry makes nothing happen: it survives
In the valley of its making where executives
Would never want to tamper . . .

        W.H. Auden, 'In Memory of W.B. Yeats'

You said to me that day,
'There's nothing you can do',
and spoke of Auden's line:
'Poetry makes nothing happen.'

        Duane Niatum, 'Consulting an Elder
        Poet on an Anti-War Poem'

Yeats got it right but not for times like these.
From quarrelling with others we shall make
Mere rhetoric, he said, while poetry's
What comes of quarrels struck up for the sake
Of psyche's anguished pleas and counter-pleas,
Its inner strife when self or soul's at stake
And conscience spurns the wish to self-appease,
Unlike the rhetorician whose big break
Comes of the perfect certainty that he's
Entirely in the right (make no mistake!)
And, granted that, self-authorized to seize
The moral high ground while the lowlands quake.

So runs the Yeatsian dictum which applies
To his work well enough since you can place
His poems on a scale that finds its highs
Where warring passions vie for psychic space,

As with his Crazy Jane when she defies
The Bishop, while its lows, in every case,
Come when some single passion clouds his eyes,
Demands he brand all others vile or base,
And gives us, lest we fail to recognize
What's good for us, a piece of in-your-face
Or rabble-rousing rhetoric in the guise
Of sentiments all readers should embrace.

Yet times there are when poets choose to stage
A private psychomachia only through
Their over-willingness to disengage
From other urgencies, a will to do
Their own soul-searching thing instead of wage
Verse-warfare of the kind the '30s crew,
Auden & Co, perceived as what the age
Required of them — after the Spanish coup
Presaged bad times ahead — and turned the page,
Pro tem at least, on all that cloud-cuckoo,
Heartfelt or morbid stuff that failed to gauge
In time just what the world was coming to.

Like it or not, that time's come round once more,
A time — Yeats saw it clearly — when 'the best
Lack all conviction' while the dogs of war,
The frauds and demagogues have repossessed
Their old terrain, dog-whistled up their core
Supporters, and made this the acid test
For poets: either keep right on with your
Verse-music meant to soothe the savage breast,
Your lyric plaints and true confessions, or
Take Brecht to heart, kick Rilke out, and rest
Assured we'll think it nothing to deplore,
That pile of juvenilia now suppressed.

Don't take it hard — just hang on till the tale
Reveals another twist as tyrants fall,
Peace reigns on Earth, the powers of good prevail,

And poets grow attentive to the call
Of lyric feelings, words that cannot fail
To move hearts wearied after the long haul
From purgatory. Still it's a trick of scale,
This sanguine view of things, and misses all
The evidence of how 'the serpent's trail
Lies over everything', how some new brawl
Of knaves or nations may yet snatch the grail
And lyric's muse grow mute beneath the pall.

A lesson here: no genre's quite as pure
As tidy-minded critics like to think,
Along with tyrants anxious to ensure
That verse and politics stay out of sync
And lyricists unwilling to endure
The harsher accents or the rancid stink
Of Juvenalian satire. Why abjure
The poet's civic role, the ancient link
Of lyric's power to move with satire's cure
For just those fond illusions that hoodwink
The purist, or exert their strongest lure
On gentle souls poised at destruction's brink?

For times there are when Yeats's sound advice —
Take issue with yourself alone, don't pick
Your fights with other people — might entice
Some tender-hearts to think of rhetoric
As lyric's sworn antagonist, the price
For headline 'relevance' achieved the quick
And dirty way; a snake in paradise
That uses every language-huckster's trick
To have sheer heft of utterance suffice
For truth. Then he who waves the biggest stick
Will pre-ensure his readers not think twice
About what ballot-slip his words might tick.

They're wrong, those lyric purists, not to see
How rhetoric's integrally a part
Of every poem, even those where we
Respect the genre-rules of lyric art,
Then blank our knowledge of them and agree
To read as if addressed straight from the heart
Without their aid. Yet what's our guarantee
That it's from there all genuine poems start,
And not from the unnoticed ministry
Of rhetoric whose workings can outsmart
The smartest rhetorician since the key,
Each time, may be a trope that flips the chart?

Clocks: A Villanelle

> *There we were in the watchmaker's shop where a host of long-case clocks, kitchen and living room clocks, alarm clocks, pocket and wrist watches were all ticking at once, just as if one clock on its own could not destroy enough time.*
>
> W.G. Sebald, *Vertigo*, trans. Michael Hulse

A few to add and time shall cease at last.
Its end creeps close with each new watch or clock.
The more I set, the more time rushes past.

Sometimes I fret lest they should tick too fast.
Why not retire, why not run down my stock?
A few to add and time shall cease at last.

A quick spot-check suffices to contrast
Their quick-change rate with my old-timer shock:
The more I set, the more time rushes past.

Freeze-framed like Wordsworth's 'stationary blast
Of waterfalls', that syncope tick-tock:
A few to add and time shall cease at last.

Let staid horologists look on aghast
As time clocks out and thought's foundations rock.
The more I set, the more time rushes past.

Watch me as I deploy my eager cast
Of time-devourers, *chronophages en bloc*:
A few to add and time shall cease at last;
The more I set, the more time rushes past.

A Wild Analysis

> *Unable to knit at the end of her life because her hands shook, Anna [Freud] mocked herself . . . for the good sublimation behaviour she had demanded of them when she was young.*
>
> *Freud called her, in one of his more daunting pieces of mythologizing, 'his Antigone.' It is one thing to be Antigone to one's father, but to be Antigone to his Movement may have been a distraction for Anna as well as a destiny. Oedipus, after all, did not start a new profession.*
>
> *Anna always hated her name, thinking of it as common and plain, while 'Sophie' [her sister's] was 'lovely and sophisticated.'*
>
> *It sounds . . . as if she was more an object of devotion than desire, and this became one of the stories of her life.*
>
> Adam Phillips, 'Anna Freud', in On Flirtation

1

I'll leave my knitting, give these hands a rest.
So taxing now, the task that once supplied
A moment's respite from the need to be
About my father's business night and day.

No doubt you analysts have second-guessed
My thought: psychosomatic, hard to hide,
That tell-tale evidence of all that he,
My father, deemed the body's price to pay

For dreams, desires or instincts long repressed,
As in the case of those perforce denied,
Like me, a life beyond the strict decree
That said 'loyal daughter' was my role to play.

It's Anna, born to serve, whom he'll invest
With that high charge: to keep them all onside,
His squabbling heirs, yet too late come to see
What costs it brought, what wishes sent astray,

What psychic torment fierce though unconfessed,
And — worst of all — how cruelly it belied
Our faith that this, the talking cure, would free
Life's victims to seek out some better way.

Always I knew he loved my sister best,
Our Sophie, his and Mama's secret pride
When, on those rare occasions, he'd agree
To let us join the social cabaret.

Yet why should I repine, why thus protest
When mine alone's the very role that I'd
Still choose if fortune offered me the key
To lives marked 'toil' or 'glitter and be gay'?

For that's the choice he, Moses-like, impressed
On me far back: how knowledge would provide
For us no pleasure-quotient such as we,
Its thankless bringers, struggled to convey.

'Your name's a palindrome!' he said, though blest
If I know how that compensates the bride
Meant not-to-be, one tutored at his knee
And quietly noting everything he'd say.

A dream long fled, that baby at my breast,
Like Sophie's Ernst, its passing classified
Amongst the lengthy list of absentee
Life-haunters logged in Father's dossier.

I've kept my life on hold at his behest,
Seen feuds enough to keep me occupied,
Fought the good fight, subdued the 'hateful me',
As Pascal said, and held that doubt at bay,

That heretic suspicion that my zest

For battling heresy declares they've died,
Those last hopes of a new world whose debris,
My whole world now, I sift through as I may.

2

Dear Anna: patient, selfless, always there
When needed, quiet, attentive, all that I,
Her father, might expect of her and yet
At times sunk in some far-off world of thought.

It's psyche's dark domain, the world we share,
Whose outer bounds I'll map before I die
If, with her aid, my explorations get
Beyond a first-time traveller's report.

Strange intimacy, something deep and rare,
I tell her constantly, though one that my
Case-histories show to hold a deeper threat:
By each Antigone the lesson's taught.

Some lives, I know, start out beyond repair
In certain ways, yet court redemption by
A life-choice made precisely to offset
Whatever ill conjunction sold them short.

What's in a name? they ask me, those who bear
A name they're easy with, that doesn't tie
Their destiny to hopes and needs unmet,
Like hers, in lifers left to hold the fort.

'Your name's a palindrome!' — I sought to spare
Her yet more anguish, but my feeble try
At consolation merely drew the net
In further as Ananke's threads grew taut.

'Same back and front', she likely thought; 'compare
My sister Sophie, apple of his eye,

With "Anna dear", his favoured epithet
For me, life-loser now turned life-support.'

I had no training: when you ask 'how dare
You analyse your daughter?', I reply,
Quite simply, that our improvised duet
Obeyed no score, set protocols at naught.

Yet turn the clock back and I'd then beware
My self-appointed privilege to pry
Into her private fantasies and let
A kinder voice prevail in that harsh court.

They call it 'wild analysis', no care
For any conscience-clause or question why
Conduct that more-than-awkward tête-à-tête
Between two lives close-knit yet stitched athwart.

'No faith but faith's undoing', we'd declare,
We two sworn infidels; yet then you'd fly,
My faithful Anna, to the parapet
Of truth and rail against the next onslaught.

I misspeak even when I say despair
Won't conquer you, for who's to testify
That it's not sheer despair but mere regret
You feel for childhood wrongs by adults wrought?

Another wrong, this botched attempt to square
Antigone's just cause with Psyche's cry
Of grief for every would-be father's pet
Whose substitute vocation's dearly bought.

Thing

The etymology of thing reveals that its abstract meanings in Old English—as 'a thought, an idea; a notion; a belief, an opinion'— come into existence alongside, even predate, its connotations as 'a material object, an article, an item; a being or entity consisting of matter, or occupying space.'

Freya Johnston, 'No Bottom to Them', *London Review of Books*, 5th December 2019, p. 44

It's a real mind-stuff puzzler, that word 'thing.'
The OED's a help: the record shows
Things change, but bygone attributes still cling.

No end to the surprises words may spring!
From inner state to stuff out there it goes.
It's a real mind-stuff puzzler, that word 'thing.'

'I feel all *thing*', you said, and made it swing
Right back to source as you or usage chose.
Things change, but bygone attributes still cling.

It's not just fetishists who catch the ring
Of old desires that object-talk bestows:
It's a real mind-stuff puzzler, that word 'thing.'

Let's think it's keener harkening that they bring,
A sense of things the object-lover knows.
Things change, but bygone attributes still cling.

Those harmonies at which the senses sing
Are what well-tuned oscillographs disclose:
It's a real mind-stuff puzzler, that word 'thing.'

For it's just there, in each vibrating string,
That sentient listeners find their highs and lows.
Things change, but bygone attributes still cling.

No fixing boundaries, no establishing
The 'it's-my-thing' to 'that thing' ratios.
It's a real mind-stuff puzzler, that word 'thing';
Things change, but bygone attributes still cling.

Martyrs of Coal*

You martyrs of coal, yours the glory
While there's still a miner alive,
Or singer to bring us the story
In which your proud legends survive.

You masters of coal, hear them calling,
Those martyrs you sent down to die,
Crushed lifeless by pit-rafters falling,
Or drowned as the waters ran high.

You martyrs, cry loud to remind us
That justice can never be done
If class-laws shall fetter and bind us
As long as the waggoners run.

You masters, you bled, starved and beat us,
You worked us to death for your gain,
You called out the troops to defeat us
And told us our strikes were in vain.

You martyrs of coal, stand beside us
As we stand today in your name
To win back the rights long denied us
And put our exploiters to shame.

And you modern masters, now hear us,
You tribe of dot-com millionaires,
Think now of their courage and fear us
When we raise the cry that was theirs.

---

* These are some English-language words I wrote to 'Merthyron y Glo', an intensely moving song with original Welsh words by Tim Saunders. It has been sung for many years by Cor Cochion Caerdydd and has music that sounds (to me) very Welsh hymn-like but which I'm told is of Eastern European origin.

For it's the same passion that fires us,
The zeal that gave courage its role,
And still their example inspires us,
Those martyrs of conscience and coal.

For Mike Billinton (1933–2019)

> Mike Billinton was a leading figure amongst what might be called the 'heroic generation' of British control-line speed fliers. His models were immaculate, finely engineered, monoline-controlled, equipped with mostly large (40 or 60 class) engines, often of all-metal construction, and always designed in highly original or ingenious ways. I have vivid recollections of him from my teenage years as a dominant presence at the Nationals and other speed events. This poem is intended by way of admiring tribute and, toward the end, melancholy reflection.

The men's stuff: 10cc control-line speed.
Time was, half-century back, when I'd be there
All day at the speed circle, hoping he'd
Get that ear-splitting model in the air.

The needle tricky, nothing guaranteed;
Successful flights spectacular but rare.
A tuned-up racing glow on bladder feed,
So called for handling with the greatest care.

Once airborne, hammering round, the thing would need
Some hanging onto, plus an outsize share
Of flying skill that visibly decreed:
'Here's how you crack those records — go compare!.'

A self-taught craftsman of the 'fifties breed
He had the skilled machinist's gifts to spare
And so, each year, contrived to supersede
His previous best for engineering flair.

Those models, metal-clad projectiles, small
(Absurdly so, with all that bhp
Up front) had wings you'd scarcely think could haul
The thing aloft and cast the dolly free.

Just an odd lap or two of groundhog crawl
Before, with luck, you'd hear the shift of key
From four- to two-stroke, and — should it not stall
On take-off — see it flying by lap three.

An engines-man at heart — just take a trawl
Through your stacked model mags and you'll agree:
It's there in all his writing, there on call,
What sorts the winner from the wannabe.

Last scene, one apt to sadden or appal,
Slow four-stroke motor, pilot all at sea,
His model earthbound, just not playing ball,
Now tracking inward on a lazy spree.

Still a fine piece of engineering, all
That you'd expect, though how explain why he,
The two-stroke wizard, let his last spell fall
On that low-revving, tame technology?

Sad truth: those latter years were spent in thrall
To Alzheimer's, which brings it home to me,
Like nothing else, how fast the blanking sprawl
Of neurons claims another absentee.

These Fuellish Things*

How people sniff when you've your flying clothes on,
The fuel-soaked handkerchief you blow your nose on,
It's you who launch my wings!
These fuellish things remind me of you.

The whiff of ether that pervades our dwelling,
The amyl nitrate that we're always smelling,
O how the magic clings!
These fuellish things remind me of you.

That prop-inflicted wound you gently cared for,
The hours of faffing that you came prepared for,
Such happy thoughts it brings!
These fuellish things remind me of you.

The screw you rescue from the grass it sinks in,
The way you tell me if the lines have kinks in,
It tugs at my heart-strings!
These fuellish things remind me of you.

That loop right after launch that barely missed you,
How you said 'sorry love' (I nearly kissed you),
Love like an engine sings!
These fuellish things remind me of you.

That little upset when the down-line dropped off,
The way you nearly got your launch-hand lopped off;
Love smiles on arms in slings!
These foolish things remind me of you.

---

* To be sung to the tune of 'These Foolish Things (Remind Me of You)', recorded by Billie Holiday in 1936. The model aircraft in question are of the control-line (or u-control) circular-flight type, rather than—like most nowadays—radio-controlled. The fuel is ether- and paraffin-based, highly aromatic, and heavy with nostalgia. The poem is dedicated to my wife and flying-partner Valerie.

The way your car smells like a Boots dispensary,
Your individual take on all things sensory,
It's there that true love springs!
These fuellish things remind me of you.

The way you angle it to keep line-tension,
The times you didn't (those we needn't mention),
Such happy circuitings!
These fuellish things remind me of you.

The flying season's here, let's check the weather,
You'll log the laps, we'll bag the bits together;
Like all of life's best things,
These fuellish things remind me of you.

Priorities

> *To'our bodies turn we then, that so*
>   *Weak men on love reveal'd may look;*
> *Love's mysteries in souls do grow,*
>   *But yet the body is his book.*
> *And if some lover, such as we,*
>   *Have heard this dialogue of one,*
> *Let him still mark us, he shall see*
>   *Small change, when we'are to bodies gone.*
>
> John Donne, 'The Ecstasy'

> *We demand that sex speak the truth . . . and we demand that it tell us our truth, or rather, the deeply buried truth of that truth about ourselves which we think we possess in our immediate consciousness.*
>
> Michel Foucault, *The History of Sexuality*

He said 'My sexual preference is tantric';
She said 'OK with me, just carry on.'
He said 'you see, I've got this little man-trick
That lets me . . . ', but by then she'd upped and gone.

Her thought: 'that Kama Sutra stuff's a winner
If ecstasy deferred is what you need,
But someone's got to get the kids their dinner,
And they've more punctual appetites to feed.'

My tip: track down the shorter (Penguin) text
We thumbed at school, check timings, choose the bits
You like the sound of, then just pick the next
Long kids-free afternoon to see what fits.

This might just get around that three-way tiff
Between your quickly satisfied desires,
The realm of soul's insatiable 'what if?',
And all that humdrum circumstance requires.

Yet take the tantric path, set work aside,
And still you'll sense the lure of that old bane,
A last hint of the body-soul divide
With sex now subtilized for spirit's gain.

Recall Spinoza, him the mystics hailed
A 'God-intoxicated soul', yet one
Who said the soul-talk simply showed we'd failed
To test how far the body's powers might run.

No need for tantric feats of self-control,
For hold-out strategies or ploys to keep
Rebellious flesh in check while offering soul
A further foothold in its mission-creep.

Much better that mild 'wisdom of the East',
Albeit customized or newly styled
For Western tastes, than some ascetic priest
Who leaves us soul-forlorn and flesh-reviled.

But better still go whole-hog Spinozist,
Embrace pure immanence, and so be freed
To find in body's remit all you missed
Through love's submission to the spirit's creed.

If soul incarnate's what you want but minus
The transcendental stuff, then you could do
Much worse than take your bearings from Aquinas
Who thought the body was the soul on view

Since mortal form is what it needs must take
To mortal eyes, a thesis that required
No bodily exactions for the sake
Of higher things to which the soul aspired.

For always there's some guru set to note
Our practices, make sure we fit the specs,
And see that we his neophytes devote
Our best endeavours to the art of sex.

What need for Grand Inquisitors when you've
Got mentors, guides, consultants, TV shows,
Live phone-ins, and a hundred ways to prove
The sex-regime has kept you on your toes.

'Keep soul-talk out of it!': the best advice,
Along with any elevated line
Of thought that offers sexual paradise
So long as body kneels at spirit's shrine.

Donne got it right: no step-change to be seen
When lovers' spirits are 'to bodies gone',
No sundered states for them to pass between
Or soul's vexed votaries to brood upon.

Bertolt Brecht: Advice to Lyric Poets

> *How can one remain free of every weakness, above all of the most deadly, of love?*
>
> *One cannot write poems about trees when the forest is full of police.*

In my poetry a rhyme
Would seem to me almost insolent.
Inside me contend
Delight at the apple tree in blossom
And horror at the house-painter's speeches.
But only the second
Drives me to my desk.

Bertolt Brecht

1

Wise up, you lyric poets, cut the crap,
Just spare us your inanities, get real,
Don't take time out while us lot take the rap.

We've heard too much about the way you feel,
That lyric sob-stuff always there on tap,
Or joy-stuff strong on heart-to-heart appeal.

Too bad if you're the moody sort who'll lap
It up from other poets, then reveal
Some inner turmoil of your own to cap

Those sad life-stories or go on to steal
The show by treating your selected scrap
Of true confession as the biggest deal.

It's what takes over when thought takes a nap,
When feeling reinvents the Petrarch wheel,
Puts love in charge, and sets the satire-trap

That's always bound to catch them by the heel,
Those soft-heads more inclined to fuss and flap
At some small tiff than where the kids' next meal

Is coming from. Just dump that lyric pap,
Go out and hit the streets — then maybe we'll
Find ways to plug the class-awareness gap.

2

Still there's another truth you'd better get
Your head around, one not flat contrary
To that but hard to square if you're dead set

On taking all your action-cues from me
And turning them straight back against the threat
Of those new fascist thugs. Forget the three-

Stage Christian trip that has lust pay its debt
To love and love to *Agape*, then see
How it's their old class-lie that has us fret

About what stage we're at. That way you'll free
The kind of comrade-love that says well-met
To every bond of trust or amity

Between those too long victimised to let
Such pious claptrap once more drown their plea
In bilge. No place for lyric warbling, yet

No hope for voices raised in any key
So harsh that Romeo and Juliet,
With all their joys and woes, can only be

Perceived as some hysterical duet
Of witless lyricists whose tragedy
Shows just how dumb those bourgeois types can get.

3

That's where their scale goes haywire at both ends
And every point between, those who declare
The love of God what utterly transcends

All other loves. Then friendship, fine though rare,
Has its subaltern role marked out and tends
To certain lesser goods that two may share,

While sexual love — whose very name offends
Agape's ear — should properly not dare
Advance its case or claim soul-dividends.

Their message: 'better use your time in prayer
Or else in making adequate amends
For sin, if you've the energy to spare,

Than causing trouble with your no-good friends,
Those god-forsaken sorts whose only care
Is to bring on some crisis that upends

The status quo.' Take that on board and they're
Yet better placed to see their power extends
Soul-deep and spreads its message everywhere

Across the echoing vault where soul now spends
Those few last lyric moments felt to bear
Whatever hopes mere privacy might lend.

4

I say it's lies they spout, those boss-class swine,
The lie that gets you workers on your knees
To big-shot monsters, human or divine,

The lie that tells the city slicker he's
Too good to waste on your production-line,

The lie that lets the bosses live at ease

While you must toil away, come shower or shine,
The lie that their lot have to bear the squeeze
Along with us, though still they wine and dine,

The lie that counts your hands-on expertise
A clear-cut wealth-and-status minus sign,
And most of all the lie that has you please

Those fat-cat celebrants of all that's fine
And heaven-blest in each lost chance to seize
Your lives back, stiffen your collective spine

And cure you finally of that disease,
The bourgeois soul. Then you'll take all the shine
Off every trick that keeps its devotees

Still worshipping at capital's fake shrine,
Self-islanded, and game for each reprise
Played out on ideology's cloud nine.

Tyche's Share

Saviour Fortune chose to sit aboard our craft so that it should neither take in the swelling surf at anchorage nor drive upon a rock-bound coast.

Aeschylus, *Agamemnon*

After I had spent some time in taking 'Kubla Khan' out of a clothes basket in successive layers like stiff and freshly laundered shirts, the dream abruptly shifted from its impish travesty of my waking efforts to a vision so lucidly clear that after the lapse of five years, as I write, it is as fresh as when I actually saw it.

J. Livingston Lowes,[*] *The Road to Xanadu*

1

No credit where no share of willed intent.
When things go well it's rarely down to your
Shrewd grasp of acts and consequences, nor,
As poems go, just saying what you meant.

Reflect a little and you'll see it's more
How things fall out than willed or heaven-sent,
The deed or word fulfilling all that went
To motivate its choice from Tyche's store.

Let's say it shows at most a certain bent,
A yen for certain trade-routes to explore
As chance affords, and from that point ignore
All tales of what-if's sunken continent.

---

[*] J. Livingston Lowes was a US literary critic whose 1927 book *The Road to Xanadu* is a remarkably detailed and erudite study of the memories, materials and verbal associations that went into the making of Coleridge's visionary poem 'Kubla Khan.' Roman Jakobson was a Czech structural linguist who first showed that the master-tropes metaphor and metonymy were central to all human language and could be used as the basis for a poetics and a typology of literary genres. Paul de Man was a highly controversial literary theorist who pressed Jakobson's distinction in a radically deconstructive direction.

Always the sense of some unopened door
That might have opened had occasion lent
You grounds enough, yet always the event
That closed it seconds, hours or years before.

Tant pis: no major cause of discontent
So long as you've that wishful thought to shore
Against the thought-worm nestling at its core
That shows your wish-account far over-spent.

2

That's what the poets and folk-heroes do
To help us out: play up to the idea
Of demiurgic powers that tell us we're,
Like them, all set to make the world anew.

The cannier types found ways to make it clear:
'Don't let us put this thing across on you;
Our pleasure-dome's a house of cards, it's true,
Our noble deeds not quite what they appear.'

For every metaphor entails a slew
Of jostling crass metonymies that veer
Off-course till timeless Symbol gets a steer
From time-bound allegory and joins the queue.

So likewise in the man-of-action sphere
Where it's the oarsmen of Odysseus' crew
That bring the mast-strapped hero safely through,
Plus wind, ship, Circe's words, and steering gear.

Let's all get high on these out-of-the-blue
Prophetic revelations, yet adhere
To prosier standards when our ship sails near
The siren reefs or caves of Xanadu.

Then our best guide to that high-risk frontier
Where visions loom is a shrewd scholar who,

Like J. Livingston Lowes, accords their due
To facts that strike the earthbound eye or ear.

3

Not quite the spirit-downer it might seem,
This proto-deconstructive will to show
What checks impede the action-man's get-go
Or humdrum details pack the poet's dream.

If it's from mundane metonyms they grow,
Those metaphors, then we've the language-scheme
Of Jakobson to level our esteem
For lyric heights and what goes on below.

Besides, as Yeats reminds us, the regime
Of metaphor and symbol may bestow
Its blessing on regimes possessed of no
Such saving grace as lets his verse redeem,

For some, the violent images that owe
Their power to sundry variants on the theme
Of how it fades, the visionary gleam,
Once *Demos* gets to shake the status quo.

A stone, he says, to vex the living stream,
Though more, I'd say, to turbulate the flow
Of Yeats's wild imagining and throw
Some metonymic shades across the beam

Of his desire that nothing spoil the show,
That words conspire to tout the fascist meme,
That syntax yield as symbol reigns supreme,
And force gives form the zealot's old heave-ho.

Fixers: Post-Election Thoughts

Now the year was twenty-twenty
And the times were looking bad,
For although the rich had plenty
They clung tight to what they had.

There were rich folk in big houses,
There were poor folk on the street,
And the rich said 'stuff your grouses,
Hit the food-banks: loads to eat!'

For the rich folk ran the shit-show
And they ran it like a dream,
Like a 'seventies pop hit-show
With a screw-the-people theme.

They fixed the courts, they fixed the press,
They fixed who made the grade,
And fixed the tax-laws so the less
You earned, the more you paid.

They sent their kids to public schools
So talking posh would hide
The fact that most were pompous fools —
Big heads with zilch inside.

They fixed the Beeb, got friends to fill
The highest admin slots,
And fixed the tales to push or kill
When boss-man called the shots.

They fixed their Tory sleepers deep
Within the Labour fold,
Those Rat-van-Winkles primed to sleep
Then squeal as they were told.

Their tales were false, their lies the kind
An idiot could see through,
Unless by some trick of the mind
That twisted thoughts askew.

But now we've got them figured out,
Wised up to all their tricks,
For though they have the money-clout
There's things that we can fix.

We'll strike, we'll fight, we'll spread dissent
And get them on the run,
For we out-match the one percent
A million-to-one.

We'll fight to save the NHS,
We'll fight to save the poor,
And if they've made your life a mess
We'll lay it at their door.

But first we'll nail the lies and crimes
Of those who pulled it off,
The monster con-trick of our times
That hatched a monster-toff.

For he's the very stuff of all
The Tory vices rolled
Into one giant-sized wrecking-ball
To leave us in the cold.

Yet still we fight, and still the swine
Hang on to what they stole,
And still the tabloids say it's fine
When gangsters take control.

So watch your backs, you devil's spawn,
You and your Eton mates,
For we've the brains as well as brawn
To pick your padlocked gates.

We'll spark revolt on your front-lawn,
Stage Putney-style debates,
And greet the day of our Red Dawn
As your day terminates.

The Eliot File

How unpleasant to meet Mr. Eliot!
With his features of clerical cut,
And his brow so grim
And his mouth so prim . . .

I am an Anglo-Catholic in religion, a classicist in literature and a royalist in politics.

Tradition . . . is of the blood, so to speak, rather than of the brain: it is the means by which the vitality of the past enriches the life of the present. In the cooperation of both is the reconciliation of thought and feeling.

> T.S. Eliot

I've got a bone or two I'd like to pick
With you, old Possum, though it's not your style,
I know, to have things out so you'll be quick
To change the subject, hedge, or run a mile
From any critic ill-advised or thick
Enough to open up the Eliot file
And ask straight out: why's no-one called his bluff,
This emperor guy parading in the buff?

Let's take your big achievements one by one
(No shortage), yet still keep in mind the kid
Who blew the gaff and spoiled the people's fun
Since he'd the confidence to lift the lid
On certain stuff that, when all's said and done,
Might be what emperor or poet hid
In plain sight lest the plebs or readers twig
How they'd been strung along by Mr Big.

Decoupling sound from sense is one technique
You use, if that's the word –more like one way
Of building up a Symbolist mystique
(Main sources: Baudelaire and Mallarmé)

By which to make your purport so oblique
That words commingle in the grey-on-grey,
Sense languishes, and poetry pursues
A sound-enchanted echolalic muse.

Let's not disparage that pitch-perfect ear
Of yours, that singing line with dying fall,
That mermaid-music from a distant sphere,
Those long-suspended cadences, and all
The quoted passages that tell us we're
From now on, willingly or not, in thrall
To one for whom 'tradition' signifies
His own choice line-up for the 'classic' prize.

Yet, this much granted, still we might decline
The proffered chance to take your guided tour
Through literary precincts where the line
Of classical descent is roughly your
Own take on it, plus liberty to mine
Those fragments ripped from context to ensure
That sounds achieve most impact with least threat
Of smart-ass readers playing hard-to-get.

The trouble is, you pushed that line so hard,
That thing about the poem's near-complete
Divorce from plain-prose reason, that we're barred,
Us bother-headed types, from crying 'cheat'
Or making extra-sure to stay on guard
Against a creed that tells us we can eat
The crumbled cake of sense but have it too
By listening out for each acoustic cue.

The poet's task, you solemnly opined,
Was not to simplify but to reflect
Those novel complications that defined
'Our present age.' Then we might re-connect
With myths and modes of being that combined
The long-fragmented shards of intellect

And feeling in a synthesis unknown
Since Shakespeare, Donne and Webster set the tone.

What drops clean out on your selective view
Of your elective forbears is the fact,
Quite simply, that they liked to think things through,
To reason, argue, get their terms exact,
Strike sparks off their conceits and not, like you,
Have euphony make up for all that's lacked
In just those conjoint qualities you prized
In them: keen wit and feeling harmonised!

Forgive me this brusque missive if it seems
A tad ungenerous, but you do strike me
As having, maybe past your wildest dreams,
So deftly fixed the major currency
Of lit-crit talk, its regnant tone and themes,
That only by lèse-majesté can we
Unwilling acolytes break free of your
Old claim to say which fragments we should shore

Against our ruin. Throwing off such rule,
One might say, 'what forgiveness?', or what hope
Of finding new direction out-of-school,
Not envying 'this man's gifts and that man's scope'
(Your words again!), but having to re-tool
And seek our own revisionary trope
By which to quiet that inner voice or quell
The workings of that Eliotic spell.

'No issue here', they'll say: 'comes down to taste,
To whether his verse-music stirs your soul
Or falls on deaf ears.' Still you're not well-placed
To side with them, considering the role
It plays in smuggling ugly or debased
Ideas and sentiments past the control
Routinely exercised by minds not apt
To flip when junk comes musically gift-wrapped.

No secret now, those muted racist slurs,
Those far-right views, that proto-fascist rot
You took from Maurras, and the beast that stirs
In phrases collocating 'Jew' and 'squat',
Anti-Semitic jibes ('money in furs'),
Or worse: 'the Jew is underneath the lot',
And all so expertly set up to prime
Receptive brains by cadence, trope, and rhyme.

It's when *Melos* gets out of touch with *Nous*
That trouble starts; when thinking takes a break
That echo's empire threatens to cut loose,
Cast rationality aside, and make
The most of any chance for mind-abuse
That junks prose sense for visceral impact's sake,
Or counts mere intellect a world well lost
When pure sound-sorcery defrays the cost.

That's how it was for you, we must allow:
The poem as (your choice) a condensate
Of having read Spinoza, and just now
Picked up the smell of cooking, plus the state
Of being in love — with no least notion how
Such oddly mixed constituents might relate
Beyond the utmost reach of human will
Or conscious thought to guide for good or ill.

Then there's the *Four Quartets*, your master-plan
For getting us ungodly types on board
Your royalist, classicist, high-Anglican,
Myth-saturated bid to strike a chord
With readers whose long-range attention span
Still leaves them over-willing to afford
Soul-space, if no room in the active brain,
For thoughts of that thought-tranquilizing strain.

Again, I'll not deny the thing has lines,
Verse-paragraphs, whole stretches that rate high

On any scale of value that confines
Itself to judging poems mainly by
The sorts of adjective applied to wines
Like rich, deep, soul-restoring (don't ask why!),
Just as a vague though fruitful tip-off lets
The pundits cite Beethoven's late quartets.

Again verse-music, but a different kind,
A flagged-up yet subliminal appeal
To works that keep your readers well in mind
Of matters spiritual and bid them feel,
Not think, their way till, sure enough, they find
Your rapt devotions urging they should kneel
At altars to a god as passing strange
As any lined up on your shooting-range.*

So when you tell us jokily that you're
'Unpleasant' or by no means nice to meet,
Then — Mr. Eliot — we had best not score
It up to mere mock-modesty but treat
It as a brief permission to explore
Things you were too repressed, or too discreet,
To say except when given half a chance
By twists of thinking, trope, or circumstance.

---

* See T.S. Eliot, *After Strange Gods: A Primer of Modern Heresy* (London: Faber & Faber, 1934)

Measure

> *In October 2018 the International Bureau of Weights and Measures voted to remove the last physical standard from the metric system, the International Prototype Kilogram, an egg-sized, platinum-iridium mass known as Le Grand K. Like other standards derived from artefacts it generated problems. In recent decades, scientists have . . . found that it was losing mass. (Though, technically, as it was the definition of the kilogram, it couldn't lose weight: the universe could only get heavier.) As of last May, the definition of a kilogram is based on Planck's constant.*
>
> James Vincent, 'As Long as the King's Arm?', *The London Review of Books*, March 5th 2020.

1

Let none declare the egg a fraction light!
Let none declare
    its mass diminished by
A zeptogram as long as it rests there.

We'd better let the yardstick rule apply.
We'd better let
    mass cosmos-wide fall square
With this one sample now the standard's set.

Be sure to cite *its* mass and you'll not err!
Be sure to cite
    the egg and you'll have met
The only test for measuring aright.

Don't go awry, let it weigh all things net.
Don't go awry
    but have scales here unite
So such anomalies don't multiply.

Yet have due care lest problems you invite.
Yet have due care
     lest physics count too high
The cost in paradox it's left to bear.

Let's just forget that stuff we quantify!
Let's just forget
     platinum eggs and dare
Go abstract so their shrinkage prove no threat.

That way we might give cosmos its due share.
That way we might
     ensure that every debt
To stuff be paid off at a single bite.

True measures lie in ghostly silhouette.
True measures lie
     past all that could requite
That old alchemic dream before we die.

It's matter's snare we spring to reach that height!
It's matter's snare,
     sprung wide, that bids us fly
Sublunary stuff with altitude to spare.

Else we'll regret not reaching for the sky.
Else we'll regret
     not sampling the pure air
Way up above the furthest wings can get.

Truths hold despite all states of disrepair.
Truths hold despite
     whatever flaws upset
Our best attempts to hold decay-rates tight.

The case shows why abstraction's our best bet.
The case shows why
     Planck's Constant is the kite-
Mark prized when stuff's too gross to reckon by.

How then compare truth's dawn with that old night?
How then compare
    those matter-based SI
Thought-hobblers with truth's answer to our prayer?

Life clamours, yet what answer's fit to try?
Life clamours, yet
    how feed such meagre fare
To those who daily face extinction's threat?

Ignore their plight, deem it a world elsewhere!
Ignore their plight
    and find them prone to fret
At fancy plans to keep them out of sight.

The human cry pleads 'quis custodiet?'
The human cry
    pleads 'who'll make good the slight
That's dealt us by the mind's inhuman eye?'

No saying they're flat wrong to pick that fight.
No saying they're
    just seeking grounds to vie
With math-based physics for the provost's chair.

The old duet, Descartes back on the sly!
The old duet,
    with that mind-sundered pair,
Mind/body, switching roles as teacher's pet.

Keep up your flight from views too doctrinaire!
Keep up your flight
    lest further wranglings let
New demons loose with every gigabyte.

2

They fix far more who fix that steady state!
They fix far more
    whose metrics may provide
Our last, best glimpse of what the mystics saw.

The abstract way takes Fibonnaci's side.
The abstract way
    bids us perceive the law
Of ratios settling what we take or pay.

The daily rate might hold large swings in store.
The daily rate
    might swing yet ratios play
Their part in ways he's quick to calculate.

Ratios abide, he taught, though tones decay.
Ratios abide
    in music just as weight
Or price marked up conceal what's bona fide.

He knew the score, kept dodgy traders straight!
He knew the score
    and sought the truth they'd hide
In scales, weights, measuring-rods, and mystic lore.

Who's then to say just where those realms divide?
Who's then to say
    where thoughts begin to soar
Beyond all commerce on the market floor?

Compare by date and see the stuff withdraw!
Compare by date
    and see the ratios stay
Intact while SI units shed their freight.

Time was they tried touchstones and moulds of clay.
Time was they tried
    Christ or some potentate
For size then divvied down or multiplied.

Always some flaw, some failure to equate.
Always some flaw
    in matter to deride
Their system and leave cheats an open door.

Back in the day they'd measure length by stride.
Back in the day
    they'd match strips to *le corps*
Glorieux then find how many strips to lay.

How estimate what errors went before?
How estimate
    those measures gone astray
For want of subtler stuff to calibrate?

Cain's fratricide kicks off the dossier.
Cain's fratricide
    has law of kind dictate
He'll then defy God's weights-and-measures guide.

In times of war fixed scales may arbitrate.
In times of war
    they keep us still supplied
With means to save some minimal rapport.

How then should they, our abstract codes, preside?
How then should they
    not tempt us to ignore
The call of those whose lifeworld they betray?

Best compensate by standing guarantor.
Best compensate
     by striving to defray
Those costs by wiping clean confusion's slate.

Why let the slide re-start once kept at bay?
Why let the slide,
     like swollen Nile in spate,
Sweep Pharaoh's body-lengths out with the tide?

A crumbling shore brings down the best flood-gate!
A crumbling shore
     lays low the fiercest pride
Of empires in one swift esturial bore.

False measures prey, chaos spreads nation-wide.
False measures prey
     on minds as shock and awe
Bid science yield once more to fortune's sway.

Love Foresworn*

I listen nightly to them as the branches sigh,
As breezes whisper through them, rumouring goodbye.
You said 'it's not for long, love, I'll be far away,
So nothing can go wrong, love, ere our wedding day.'
Yet still I hear them weeping,
That threnody unsleeping,
Their constant vigil keeping as the moments fly;
Their constant vigil keeping as the moments fly.

You said our love would hold me safe beneath its wing,
Our loving vows enfold me like a wedding ring.
O how your words still calm me, words so sweet and kind,
So I ask what could harm me though I stay behind.
But then the trees awaken,
I feel their branches shaken,
And fear myself forsaken in the sound they bring;
And fear myself forsaken in the sound they bring.

O would you'd spoken truly when you turned to go.
Those words now echo cruelly when the night-winds blow.
You promised me we'd soon be back together, dear,
So when the crescent moon returned she'd find us here.
Yet then the doubt comes preying,
Your kindly words unsaying,
And restless branches swaying as the shadows grow;
And restless branches swaying as the shadows grow.

It's not the moon to blame, love, though it wax and wane,
It's you who never came, love, when I cried in vain.
Their rustling said you'd met some new love as you went
And my betrayal set their leaves in wild lament.
But as their tumult swelling

---

* This is a song-lyric written to fit the melody of Dvorak's Slavonic Dance Op. 78, No. 2 in D minor. It is a beautiful piece which I hear as chiefly wistful, subdued, even melancholy in character, though of course other listeners may respond differently. The narrative and bitter ending are entirely invented.

Declares a grief past telling
I'll make the woods my dwelling lest you come again.
I'll make the woods my dwelling lest you come again.

Yet now the nights are longer and the wind blows chill,
And thoughts of you run stronger as I wait here still.
I wanted to forgive you, let you wander free,
Say 'it's your life to live, you once so dear to me.'
But now those words ring fake, love,
Not worth the sound they make, love,
And so for pity's sake, love, wander where you will.
And so for pity's sake, love, wander where you will.

Vermin

But, by what I have gathered from your own Relation, and the Answers I have with much Pains wringed and extorted from you, I cannot but conclude the Bulk of your Natives, to be the most pernicious Race of Little odious Vermin that Nature ever suffered to crawl upon the Surface of the Earth.

King of Brobdingnag, in Jonathan Swift,
Gulliver's Travels, Part 2, Chapter 6

This is always likely to happen; everything spiritual and valuable has a gross and revolting parody, very similar to it, with the same name; only unremitting effort can distinguish between them, as with Swift.

William Empson, *Some Versions of Pastoral*

As Gulliver stays with the Houyhnhnms, he comes to detest his own kind, flinching to see his own face in a lake. When at last he must leave, he feels he is going into exile. But of course he is now taken back to Europe and eventually returns to his family. Life in England seems exile indeed. Here, reason, which should unite men, keeps them apart. Gulliver thinks now of living as a recluse, i.e., like an isolated prisoner, cut off from mankind. But finally he does not.

Irvin Ehrenpreis: *Swift: the man, his works and the age*, Vol. 3

1

Who'll then gainsay the atrabilious Swift?
He's tried all sorts and sizes, then declared
We're vermin: how resist his cynic drift?

The gentle giants supply a short-term lift
Until we non-giants see we'll not be spared:
Who'll then gainsay the atrabilious Swift?

No human vice but found its symptoms sniffed
Out and personified, its vileness shared.
Just vermin: how resist his cynic drift?

A Midas touch, that conscience-flaying gift
Of his that leaves our every weakness bared.
Who'll then gainsay the atrabilious Swift?

There's none escape the misanthrope's short-shrift,
His mirror-trap that has all readers snared.
Mere vermin: how resist the cynic drift?

No point our acting up or feeling miffed
At finding our most secret vices aired.
Who'll then gainsay the atrabilious Swift?

It drove him mad, that flesh-engendered rift
With soul, that perfect circle crudely squared.
Just vermin: how resist his cynic drift?

Big/small, good/bad: it's when perspectives shift
We find ourselves bewildered, unprepared.
Who'll then gainsay the atrabilious Swift?

From Swift to Hopkins, it's the same 'soft sift
In an hourglass' refrain that has us scared,
Us vermin: how resist his cynic drift?

A start: wise up to signs of verbal grift,
Of puns on 'spirit' ribald as he dared.
You'll not gainsay the atrabilious Swift
But shield us vermin, curb his cynic drift.

2

So cunningly he plots the double-bind!
Pull either way, you'll feel the reef-knot squeeze.
No wriggling free, for you or humankind.

The reasoning Houyhnhnms whinnied, looked, and dined
Like horses yet discoursed like Socrates:
So cunningly he plots the double-bind!

Poor Gulliver could only lag behind
When tutored in his civic abc's.
No wriggling free, for him or humankind.

How keep his cool when mortified to find
They classed him with their brute antitheses?
So cunningly Swift plots the double-bind!

The Yahoos, shaggy humanoids, declined
All bids to raise them horse-ward by degrees:
No wriggling free, for them or humankind.

Appalled, he watched them joyfully unwind
By dumping dung on Houyhnhnms from the trees.
So cunningly Swift plots the double-bind!

The message clear, 'tu quoque' underlined:
For conspecifics, take a look at these!
No wriggling free, for him or humankind.

You wonder: was he wholly sound of mind,
Dean Swift, to play that exit-blocking wheeze
So cunningly and plot the double-bind?

For there's self-hatred everywhere entwined
With his high scorn for others' slime and sleaze:
No wriggling free, for him or humankind.

What if his zeal for satire leaves him blind
To symptoms of that creeping hate-disease
As cunningly he plots the double-bind?

Then all those shrewd contrivances designed
To box us in will go to show that he's
Less wriggle-room than most of humankind,
Though cunningly he plots their double-bind.

3

Three centuries on and who'll refute the Dean?
Now Yahoos rule and Houyhnhnms ruminate.
Let cynics thrive in the Anthropocene!

Though choleric his gibes cut quick and clean
Now fuckwit pirates steer the ship of state.
Three centuries on and who'll refute the Dean?

Don't think to censor such displays of spleen
As icecaps melt and floes disintegrate.
Let cynics thrive in the Anthropocene!

The misanthrope alone has strictures keen
And consequent enough to tell us straight:
'Three centuries on and who'll refute the Dean?.'

Why puzzle what such ironies could mean
At this last stage in time, this endgame date?
Let cynics thrive in the Anthropocene!

'Poor Swift', they used to say, 'strung out between
The threefold kinds of love, the one of hate.'
Three centuries on and who'll refute the Dean?

For sure not those whose hopes, once evergreen,
Now turn sere-yellow as the time grows late.
Let cynics thrive in the Anthropocene!

Time was they thought he'd copped a faulty gene,
Had childhood fears or sins to expiate:
Three centuries on and who'll refute the Dean?

They strike us every day from page and screen,
The global images that spell our fate:
Let cynics thrive in the Anthropocene!

Why ask that tact or good taste intervene?
Just turn on us the horrors we create!
Three centuries on and who'll refute the Dean?

The warnings stark, the wake-up calls routine;
No time for rules of civilized debate.
Let cynics thrive in the Anthropocene!
Three centuries on and who'll refute the Dean?

4

How should not *anthropos* turn foe to man?
By Book Four Swift and Lemuel muse in sync.
'Hate all alike': the misanthrope's best plan.

Size up, size down — that's how his tale began,
The small guys nasty, big guys apt to stink.
How should not *anthropos* turn foe to man!

Kids' stuff, that bigger-than and smaller-than;
No threat when it's just bodies stretch or shrink.
'Hate all alike': the misanthrope's best plan.

It's when the rule necessitates they scan
Their ownmost faults that satirists may blink:
How should not *anthropos* turn foe to man?

Then rancour spreads past rival, tribe or clan
To all mankind through that infernal chink.
'Hate all alike': the misanthrope's best plan.

Just score max points for nasty when you can,
Out-scourge all comers, crush the weaker link:
How should not *anthropos* turn foe to man?

Let Prospero yield his staff to Caliban,
The satyr give the sage a crafty wink.
'Hate all alike': the misanthrope's best plan.

Show hunchback Pope he's a mere also-ran,
Too mild for those poised on extinction's brink.
How should not *anthropos* turn foe to man?

Just shove his well-turned couplets down the pan
As fear pulls tight on every psychic kink.
'Hate all alike': the misanthrope's best plan.

Let Swiftian rage spark clean across the span
Of years as oceans rise and forests shrink.
How should not *anthropos* turn foe to man?

It's desperate times put satire in the van,
Bid mockery thrive as hopes and empires sink.
'Hate all alike': the misanthrope's best plan.
How should not *anthropos* turn foe to man?

5

Don't fear to hack it, that last branch you've got.
Keep chopping when they chide 'stay put and fight!.'
Why think your hanging on will stop the rot?

The Swiftian fix: how put them on the spot,
Those sundry rogues and fools, while you sit tight?
Don't fear to hack it, that last branch you've got.

The blowback bit is where Swift lost the plot,
Where moral stricture turned to moral blight.
Why think your hanging on will stop the rot?

If you, the baiter, share your species-slot
With those you bait it's your own hand you bite:
Don't fear to hack it, that last branch you've got.

Safe hands keep satire to some aliquot
Of target-readers wise to what they write.
Why think such hanging-on will stop the rot?

See how those shrewd precautions go to pot
As unchecked hatred blocks the line of sight.
Don't fear to hack it, that last branch you've got.

Count yourself out, just nail the other lot,
And hear the howls of hatred you'll invite.
Why think just hanging on will stop the rot?

It's yours, the pristine copy-book you'll blot,
Self-cast as Abdiel, lone against the night.
Don't fear to hack it, that last branch you've got.

Too like the Yahoos, too inclined to squat
In trees and dump on Houyhnhnms from a height.
Why think just hanging on will stop the rot?

And more: the satire gets too scattershot
When self-love, not self-knowledge, points the spite:
Don't fear to hack it, that last branch you've got.

Just hack right through and then we'll see you've not
Perchance looked down and nearly died of fright.
Why think just hanging on will stop the rot?

Though others' vices must loom large in what
You satirise, still it's for you to smite
And hack away at that last branch you've got
Beneath you: hanging on won't stop the rot!

Elements

For Edward Greenwood

For by Art is created that great LEVIATHAN called a COMMON-WEALTH, or STATE, which is but an Artificial Man; though of greater stature and strength than the Natural, for whose protection and defence it was intended; and in which, the Sovereignty is an Artificial Soul, as giving life and motion to the whole body.

Thomas Hobbes, *Leviathan*

Being in a gentleman's library, Euclid's Elements lay open . . . . [Hobbes] read the proposition 47. By G—,' sayd he, 'this is impossible!' So he reads the demonstration of it, which referred him back to such a proposition; which proposition he read. That referred him back to another, which he also read. Et sic deinceps, that at last he was demonstratively convinced of that truth. This made him in love with geometry.

After he began to reflect on the interest of the king of England as touching his affairs between him and the parliament, for ten years together his thoughts were much, or almost altogether, unhinged from the mathematiques; but chiefly intent on his De Cive, and after that on his Leviathan: which was a great putt-back to his mathematical improvement..

John Aubrey, A *Brief Life of Thomas Hobbes, 1588-1679*

'By God', I cried, 'this reasoning cannot hold!'
(God witness, it's for emphasis I'd swear.)
'May not the greatest thinkers sometimes err?
The proposition stinks, if truth be told.'
But then I saw the *Elements* unfold,
Found truth conserved, the geometry foursquare,
The logic faultless, and, shown everywhere,
The *a priori* knowledge that consoled
A contumelious mind. 'Such forceless force

Of logic, how it brings us worms to know
Those certain truths thrown up in reason's course,
All set out *more geometrico*
And thus requiring all men to endorse
Them without question or let logic go.'

From that rapt moment on I sought to share
Its tumult-quelling gift with all who'd stow
Their grievances, avert the body blow
Of civil war, take counsel, and declare
Themselves of reason's party *après-guerre*,
Hence resolute to let no conflict throw
Such transient fallings-out into the flow
Of logic's elements as they progress to their
Resistless q.e.d. How not abate
Those noxious feuds, that chaos come again,
Those late debaucheries of Church and State,
When Euclid sets his case out pikestaff-plain
In close-linked axioms fit to demonstrate
Their truth even to my befuddled brain.

I wrote my book *Leviathan* to teach
Those sectaries the error of their ways,
To lead them by example through the maze
Of falsehoods spread by zealots out to preach
Sedition and the anarch's code of each
Man his own conscience, qualified to raise
A schism, creed, or army, or — in days
Not long gone by — a monstrous gaping breach
In reason's commonwealth. Let *cives* learn
From geometer not prelate, statesman take
A course in axiomatics, preacher turn
To Euclid for instruction — then they'll make
Good all the damage done by those who spurn
The way of truth for private passion's sake.

Truth absolute, indubitable, shown
By formal proof, and thereby proof against

Mob sentiment, unreason, brains incensed
By ranting oratory, rebellion grown
To compass regicide — it's that alone,
That one sure anchor-point, that recompensed
Whole ages of stupidity condensed
In the phrase 'civil war' whose gist I groan
Once more to recollect. A forlorn hope,
I sometimes think, my bookish quest to coax
The zealots down, have calmer passions cope
In such wild times when reason's voice provokes
Rekindled strife. Yet soon enough I'll grope
My next inch forward despite the taunts and jokes.

They're prey to phantasms, to all the tricks
And shape-shift sorceries that craze the mind
When Proteus meddles with the laws of kind,
Sets men at odds, confounds their politics,
And looses on them that unholy mix
Of party, faith and avarice combined
That leaves Leviathan compelled to find,
Sans sovereign reason, other ways to fix
Its storm-tossed voyaging. Then, to be sure,
Unending motion holds the only key
To minds as well as bodies; thoughts endure
No more than shapes or sizes, and if we
Think otherwise it's only till the lure
Of motion drives us whales back out to sea.

My death draws nigh and says 'Don't be afraid',
Which counsel now, *aetatis* eighty-four,
I take to heart and cherish all the more
For having lived by reason's light and made,
As best I could, its rule the one that weighed
Most strongly with me since inclined to draw,
In those my books, sound lessons from the store
Of ancient precedents now aptly laid
Before our warring tribes. As bodies yield
To intellect, so they must yield to laws

Prescribed, and rightly so, by those who wield
The sovereign power to separate just cause
From unjust, act as Everyman's best shield,
And keep Leviathan from Satan's jaws.

To Malmesbury I'll soon return and die,
Perhaps, with childhood landmarks clear in view,
The ancient monastery and castle, two
Fine citadels of Church and State, set high
On that opposing hillside and, to my
Mind even then, each with its power to do
Great good or harm; trust reason and stay true
To virtue's cause or further amplify
Our discords lately quelled. For nothing stirs
The blood to faction, feud and all the woes
Of civil war like powers abused, nor spurs
The virtuous mind more firmly to oppose
War's evils than the insight that confers
Such peace as civic geometry bestows.

Yet I've no ready answer, none to quiet
Their taunts or my own doubts, when sceptics mock
My thought that Euclid's proofs might ease the shock
Of civil strife, cool hotheads ere they riot,
Bring social peace through change of mental diet,
Or — sheer absurdity! — provide a rock
Of shared assent for those inclined to knock
The block off any party who won't buy it
When they dictate what's what. And there's the fact,
Much dwelt on by those carpers, that so far
From lying low, preferring thought to act,
And hiding in my study lest I mar
The Euclid moment, I've at no time lacked
For worldly ways to chase Dame Fortune's star.

Nor should they count me fool enough to think
It might, that moment, somehow overleap
The confine of my skull and swiftly creep,

As if by occult medium, link by link,
Into the skulls of those caught on the brink
Of civil war, contriving thus to keep
Their nations free of all that else might sweep
Whole polities to limbo in a blink
Of its Cyclopic eye. What might the name
'Hobbes' signify, in popular repute,
If not the wicked infidel whose aim
Is to relinquish mind and soul to brute
Materiality, and who'd proclaim
Such mystic notions kids' stuff to refute?

That gets me wrong, flat wrong, but I'll concede
One point: there's no royal road, nor (if you please)
Republican thought-highway fit to ease
My contrarieties, my twofold need
That civic order take the form decreed
By reason's rule and, as I see in these
Bad times, that no fake nostrum claim to ease
The restless passions chafing to stampede
In all men, me not least. They'll read my works
In times to come, those scholars, and enquire
What demon drove me on, what tumult lurks
Behind the Euclid-tale they so admire,
Or why that soothing anecdote still irks
One lured as much by reason as desire.

Life and Logic: An Agon (Frege)

Desperate, lonely, cut off from the human community which in many cases has ceased to exist, wracked by desires for intimacy they do not know how to fulfil, at the same time tormented by the presence of women, men turn to logic.

The philosopher who combs the tangles from language must also be a butcher who trims away the fleshy fat of ordinary talk to leave the bare bones of truth.

Andrea Nye, *Words of Power: a feminist reading of the history of logic*

1

The noises start each time I turn away.
As symbols fill the blackboard so the air
Fills with my students' mockery. I bear
It without protest, hate them as I may.

The truths are hard, the insights all too rare.
How thoughts conspire to lead themselves astray!
It's truth alone keeps error's hordes at bay;
Let logic hear no more of feeling's share.

First target: natural language, where the sway
Of sentiment's a hazard to beware
Lest, using words without sufficient care,
We think amiss and there's a price to pay.

Confusing terms is one sure way to err,
Like 'concept' and 'idea', so you betray —
Like those fool students — how an everyday
Speech-habit proves a thought-disabling snare.

It's meanings merely private they convey
When speaking of 'ideas', thus showing they're

So far off-track that sometimes I despair
Of setting straight such mental disarray.

Ideas, like feelings, are one's own affair,
The sorts of fuzzy mental stuff that they,
Those students, might get by on as they play
Their games and whisper loudly as they dare.

No matter! It's thought's groundwork I must lay,
Its logical foundations, clean and spare,
No excess flesh, no feelings to declare
('Poor Gottlob, what a loveless life!', they say).

I see them, students, colleagues, pair by pair.
They live and love, but to what purpose, pray?
Make truth your idol, and those feet of clay,
Turned hard, will keep thought's superstructure square.

2

Not love but hatred, hate of all things skewed,
Illogical, emotive, vague, unclear,
Or plain deluded, like that crazed idea
Of Heidegger that truth might spring from mood.

Thoughts harden lest emotions interfere
Or feelings cloud their lucid solitude.
My jest: that 'student' signifies 'one stewed
In a thick soup of sentiment and beer.'

They'll find my journals one day, call them 'crude',
'Misogynist' and 'racist', try to smear
My character and even say that we're
All crazed, all us logicians — monstrous brood!

And more: they'll seize on every chance to sneer
At me as just another badly screwed-
Up anti-semite, one whose bitter feud
With rivals morphed into a street-mob jeer.

What care I if my life-work's now construed,
In their crass terms, as stemming from my fear
Of women, proto-fascist traits, or mere
Logician's terror lest the world intrude?

I sense them massing now on thought's frontier,
Those soft-brain liberal 'reformers' who'd
Convince us their fake nostrums yield more food
For thought than logic — doctrine too severe!

It's crystalline perfection I've pursued,
A thinking ultra-hard and mind austere
Enough to hold, within its crystal sphere,
Truths valid from whatever angle viewed.

Sometimes I wonder what if I held dear
Those things they love, those pleasures I've eschewed
For logic's sake; then swiftly I conclude:
Subdue the flesh till logic's bones show clear!

Politics and Poetry: two views

1

They ask me: why the antique style?
Why have them rhyme and scan?
Why fiddle while Rome burns, or while
Our lives go down the pan?

It's rough-house stuff, the stuff we need,
Red-hot with scorn and rage,
Not stuff for owlish types to read
Off some age-yellowed page.

Just cut the crap, let feeling loose,
And let those bastards know
Their fancy ways will be no use
When us lot run the show.

We'll stuff their art-forms up their arse,
Run riot with their rhymes,
And turn their tragedies to farce
As suits these squalid times.

Just drop the archaisms, drop
The Pope-and-Dryden bit;
They'll let you take a gentle pop
But never score a hit.

So stick with us, let form go hang,
Jump up and grab the mike;
That way you'll get the biggest bang
And give us what we like.

2

Point taken, but one thing you've missed,
You lords of verse misrule,
Is how the canny formalist
Stays hot while staying cool.

It's rhyme and meter, they're the way
Verse-satire takes its aim,
Like cross-hair sights whose sharp display
Shows where to fix the blame.

All well and good, your scatter-shot,
One hit will up your score
But more than likely see you pot
A good half-dozen more.

With formal verse you're set to strike
Just how and whom you will,
Your techniques honed word-perfect like
A skilled machinist's drill.

You fix your sights, then make your choice:
Which set-up works the best?
What meter, rhyme-scheme, tone of voice,
Which vices duly stressed?

That's how you channel and contain
The wish to knock them dead;
By letting satire take the strain,
Not kicks aimed boot-to-head.

Après-Coup

This violent praxis is totalizing since each individual represents a violent link in the great chain, in the almighty body of violence rearing up in reaction to the primary violence of the colonizer.

Because it is a systematic negation of the other person and a furious determination to deny the other person all attributes of humanity, colonialism forces the people it dominates to ask themselves the question constantly: 'In reality, who am I?.' The defensive attitudes created by this violent bringing together of the colonised man and the colonial system form themselves into a structure which then reveals the colonised personality.

  Frantz Fanon, *The Wretched of the Earth*

Get this into your head: if violence were only a thing of the future, if exploitation and oppression never existed on earth, perhaps displays of nonviolence might relieve the conflict. But if the entire regime, even your nonviolent thoughts, is governed by a thousand-year old oppression, your passiveness serves no other purpose but to put you on the side of the oppressors.

  Jean-Paul Sartre, Preface to *The Wretched of the Earth*

Each comes to me, each comes with his own tale,
The tortured and the torturer, and I,
Their shrink-confessor, hear them out and try
To draw aside the post-traumatic veil
Of roles reversed that has guilt-feelings flail
The victims while tormentors testify,
In anguished tones, to the wrongs done them by
Those same accusers whom fresh doubts assail
As each charge echoes back. My thinking: strive
For some small space or foothold whence to find,
For tortured souls, their best chance to survive
Renewed assaults of that most deadly kind
And, for the guilty, ways to keep alive
The scenes they'd striven not to keep in mind.

Freud tells us how such hellish couplings thrive
On hatred and survivor-guilt combined,
How deep it goes when lives are intertwined
With horrors once the routine nine-to-five
Of one man's work now jostling to connive
With the other's fear and, from that daily grind,
Project a future scene with roles assigned
To psychic forces locked in overdrive
By civil war. My role: to hold the scale,
A shaky Rhadamanthus, trust to my
Twin mentors, Freud and Sartre, and derail
Ahead of time those memory-trains that ply
Unconscious depths lest censorship should fail
And chunks of mental wreckage streak the sky.

We know the mechanism, one that he,
The Marxist-existentialist, laid bare:
How torturers and anti-semites share
The same perverse compulsion first to flee,
Then hurt, then kill those whom they take to be
Sheer Other, alien to them and their
Most cherished values, though the truth they bear,
Those victims, witnesses the human plea
For justice, love and peace. Who better showed
Their workings, all the mazy ways and means
By which bad faith found pretexts to offload
Its guilt-account, or conscience found routines
To catechize the torturer who'd stowed
Them well away, those ego-censored scenes.

My charge: to tend them both, to lend an ear,
To harken in that special, fine-tuned way
Of psychoanalysts to what they say,
Or don't say, as the cues and clues appear
In their entangled discourses and we're
Required, as good practitioners, to stay
Quite neutral, not by the least hint betray
Whatever we may think or feel for fear

Of driving them to silence. So it runs,
The stock clinician's rule, and so I make
My Freudian vow each time, though it's the ones
With comrades' life-blood on their hands who take
Most coping with if I envisage guns
And thumbscrews when they plead 'For pity's sake.'

They pull me both ways, Sartre with his stress
On choice and freewill, his resolve to bar
All pleas for the defence that ease ajar
The creaky back-door marked 'under duress',
And Freud with his exemplary largesse
In taking human creatures as they are,
All victims, all tormentors, none so far
From his stock counterpart as rules we bless
The one and curse the other. I've sat through
Long sessions with the torturers who said,
'Sincerely' as it goes, that though they'd do
The same next time around they'd seen the dead
And mutilated in their dreams and knew
Too well why revenants should bring such dread.

To Sartre I'd say: so glad you thought again,
Played down the theme of freedom absolute,
That faddish *rive gauche* bourgeois attribute,
And saw its scope diminish sharply when
The question was: in times of war, what then?
How say you freely suffer it, that boot
Drawn back to smash your face, or freely shoot,
Though pacifist, the sniper with your men
Square in his sights? It's where that notion met
Its nemesis, the shrinking space assigned
For suchlike freedom-talk when conflicts get
Close up and dirty, civil discords bind
The warring parties, and the action's set
To run till death perfects their double-blind.

To Freud: no *mise-en-scène*, no civil war
More fierce — you'd have us know — than those that filled
Your case-book histories, the psyches drilled
In self-tormenting ways whose wrongs implore
Our grief but some with wrongs to answer for,
The torturers whose crimes were scarcely willed,
As willing goes, but followed rules instilled
At gunpoint, orders no-one could ignore
Unless on pain of death. It's what I took
From you, that lesson in the moral luck
That shapes our ends, the ill-kept ledger-book
Where accidents conspire to push the buck
Far back from where those first-stone-casters look
Who'd leave the miscreant no room to duck.

They come, they talk, I draw them out, provide
What help I can to those who'd sooner lock
The door on thoughts from their infernal stock,
Thoughts that could leave them suddenly wild-eyed
With fear, or grief, or guilt, or states that I'd
No word for since their violence seemed to knock
A hole in my shrink's manual, or to mock
All hopes they might be filed and classified
Amongst its specimens. Only through late-
Stage, fleeting intimations might I know,
Or safely guess, which party bore most weight
Of self-contempt, which way the case might go,
Or who'd present as guilt-racked candidate
For grace and who'd endure the torturer's blow
Once more each time around, as if to state
That psyche's law can only mean death-row.

And I, the one tasked every day to bring
An expert's ear and mind, a judgment void
Of fear or favour, like the elder Freud,
Beyond our own or pleasure's reckoning —
How live the stranger's role that has me cling
To words and manner barely humanoid,

My mentors' keenest insights now deployed
To draw, not point, the promissory sting
Of such hard teachings. So I hear them all,
The Berbers and the *pieds-noirs*, colonists
And colonised, poor Arab and rich Gaul,
And share the torments as my role insists,
Yet note how quickly words translate the brawl
From army, hit-squad, rifle, knife, or fists
To the dark combat-zone of minds in thrall
To other, more elusive pugilists.

Rhyme and Rote: A Caesurelle*

> *A vast portion of verbal behaviour consists of recurrent patterns, of linguistic routines including the full range of utterances that acquire conventional significance for an individual, group or whole culture.*
>
> Dell Hymes

> *A considerable proportion of our everyday language is 'formulaic.' It is predictable in form and idiomatic, and seems to be stored in fixed, or semi-fixed, chunks . . . . [It involves] our use of prefabricated material which, although less flexible, also requires less processing.*
>
> Alison Wray

> *Rhyme I would say is a kind of metaphor—a likeness between unlikes—and has some of the same mysterious power. It is a driver of composition and not an ornament (if done properly)—a rhymed poem should, in a sense, be 'rhyme-driven.'*
>
> A. E. Stallings

Words come *en bloc*, or so the linguists say.
Words come *en bloc*,
    not one by one as thought
Unfolds, but as birds vanish in a flock.

Whole days go by in mind-states of that sort.
Whole days go by
    with nothing apt to knock
Them out of custom's rut before we die.

---

* Note: 'caesurelle' is my term for a verse-form invented by William Empson but used by him on just one occasion, in his poem 'The Teasers.' He thought the poem a failure but the form a lovely invention; I disagree about the poem but very much agree about the form, which I have employed many times. 'Caesurelle' seems an apt enough name given what sounds like (though isn't, strictly speaking) a caesura in the second/third line of each stanza.

The price we pay is dealing in old stock.
The price we pay
     is then our need to ply
A trade in stuff that's long since had its day.

'Keep thought-lines taut' is one hop-up to try.
'Keep thought-lines taut'
     so sense won't leak away
Or fade for lack of intellect's support.

Keep things adhoc, keep thought-routines at bay.
Keep things adhoc
     and don't sell thinking short
Like nifty craft too long laid up in dock.

Rhyme lets words fly, hits volleys way off-court!
Rhyme lets words fly
     while meter springs the lock
That closed their wings before they touched the sky.

Give block-cliché that rhyme-engendered shock!
Give block-cliché
     a chance to wing it high
As thinking goes creatively astray.

Else you'll be caught in custom's language-sty.
Else you'll be caught,
     link words up as you may,
With no way out save habit's stock retort.

From tick to tock it's in dead time you'll play.
From tick to tock
     with senses dulled to thwart
Your wish for kerygmatic time to clock.

How then untie word clusters custom-wrought?
How then untie
      what holds our thought in hock
To autocues that catch our mental eye?

Speech-habits lay down spoilers, chock by chock.
Speech-habits lay
      them down unless we try
What means we have to blue the grey-on-grey.

They say 'abort this take-off, don't ask why!'
They say 'abort',
      but we say 'why obey
If one spry rhyme can jump the juggernaut?.'

Macaque

> *At the Uluwatu temple in Bali, monkeys mean business. The long-tailed macaques are infamous for brazenly robbing tourists and clinging on to their possessions until food is offered as ransom payment. . . . Shrewd macaques prefer to target items that humans are most likely to exchange for food, such as electronics, rather than objects that tourists care less about. . . . Bargaining between a monkey robber, tourist and a temple staff member often lasted several minutes. The longest wait before an item was returned was twenty-five minutes, including seventeen minutes of negotiation.*
>
> Rebecca Ratcliffe, *The Guardian*, 14th January 2021

No flies on me, the super-smart macaque,
So quick to spot the priciest tourist gear!
There's aeons of culture-goods want paying back.

The phones and cameras, they're the things to track,
The kind of stuff those tourist-types hold dear.
No flies on me, the super-smart macaque!

See that new-model, top-range camera pack?
Size the guy up, check the escape-route's clear.
There's aeons of culture-goods want paying back.

Shan't settle for some piece of bric-a-brac,
Cheap handkerchief or temple souvenir:
No flies on me, the super-smart macaque.

Best get a tame staff-member to fast-track
The business side, give things a timely steer:
There's aeons of culture-goods want paying back.

Drive the rate up: that mobile's worth a snack
More generous than what's on offer here.
No flies on me, the super-smart macaque!

Hold out five minutes longer and they'll crack,
Say 'name your price!' to please me out of fear
There's aeons of culture-goods want paying back.

If those poor fools could only learn the knack
Of bartering my snacks would be small beer:
No flies on me, the super-smart macaque.

A full half-hour I'll keep them on the rack,
Display the spoils, enjoy the chance to jeer:
There's aeons of culture-goods want paying back.

Treat-wise, their mobiles keep me in the black
While nifty cameras bring me daylong cheer.
No flies on me, the super-smart macaque.

And should the tourist horde lament my lack
Of morals then I'll mock their venal tear:
There's aeons of culture-goods want paying back;
No flies on me, the super-smart macaque!

Ernesto Cardenal (1925–2020)*

With lowered head you met him, Pope John Paul.
With lowered head
      but mind and heart held high:
His gospel darkest blue, yours deepest red.

No chance you'd hit it off, meet eye-to-eye.
No chance you'd hit
      some middling path to tread
And reconcile that all-too-public split.

Your gospel call was 'give the hungry bread.'
Your gospel call
      was: hear the poor man's cry
And feed the spirit when there's bread for all.

Pie-in-the-sky, that other-worldly bit.
Pie-in-the-sky
      so long as faith played ball
With US firms that bled your people dry.

'Faith first', he said, 'else into sin you'll fall.'
'Faith first', he said,
      'and don't rush to apply

---

* Ernesto Cardenal, who died on March 1, 2020, was a Nicaraguan poet, Marxist, Catholic priest and lifelong left activist who fought a protracted campaign against the more conservative wing of Catholic religious and social doctrine. When Pope John Paul visited Managua in 1993 Cardenal famously knelt before him on the runway but was rebuffed and told to mend his dissident ways. His relations with Daniel Ortega's Sandinista government were strained in later years but Cardenal was active in the overthrow of Somoza, remained deeply committed to the revolution, and served for a time as Minister of Culture (a role John Paul placed high on the charge-sheet). His renegade status was only revoked and Cardenal's full priestly office restored in 2019 by the 'liberal' Pope Francis.

Cardenal's poetry always united the lyrical and passionate with the tough-minded and political, though it moved increasingly in the latter direction. At best it displays a Brechtian combination of factual nitty-gritty, heartfelt social protest, and a gift for placing vividly evocative image and metaphor in the service of both poetic aims.

That social creed lest folk should be misled.'

You'd holy writ on which to testify.
You'd holy writ
      to back that creed and spread
Home-truths John Paul would shudder to admit.

If they appal, those truths, then act instead!
If they appal
      (you challenged him) then why
Let faith erase that writing on the wall?

You nailed the lie that called their crimes legit.
You nailed the lie
      that made weak brethren crawl
To those your poems urged they should defy.

Too long in bed with hucksters great and small.
Too long in bed,
      his Church, with those who'd pry
And fix elections when their strong-man fled.

Much better quit, you told the Fruit Corp guy.
Much better quit
      or have their assets bled
And crimes revealed with penalties to fit.

It's capital whose curse we have to shed.
It's capital,
      you wrote, that dares deny
Christ's message and have Paul revert to Saul.

We'll scan it by the Marxist lights you lit.
We'll scan it by
      reviewing faith's long haul
With optics set to 'life before we die.'

Two Books

Two books at any given time I keep
Always to hand, both there each time I wake,
And then again before I go to sleep,
Pen poised for any notes I want to take.

The one's a book of poems I admire,
Or love, or count 'a major influence', or
Place high amongst the models I'd aspire
To match if mine jumped twenty notches more.

The favourites multiply, the choice rotates,
As new discoveries pile up one by one
And Auden, Bishop, Larkin, Empson, Yeats
Are joined by Wilbur, Murray, Moore and Gunn.

They size me up, they keep me on my toes,
And should I feel the slightest touch of pride
In any verse of mine they soon disclose,
By contrast, all the faults I'd hoped to hide.

But there's the other books, my favourites too,
Though (shamefully) hand-picked to let me think
'Thank God for that — at least the stuff I do
Looks good compared with Cloth-Eared Scribblers Inc.'

No names, of course, since they're the blessed props
That hold me upright when the alpha-grade
Exemplars hit me, lest the penny drops:
Best junk your efforts, learn another trade!

For it's by their good offices you learn
How halting lines, verse-rhythms so inept
They trip you up, stock phrases, rhymes that earn
The Stuffed Owl prize, whole chunks the poet slept

Or lurched their way through — all may serve to show,
Like misspent youth, that yours is not a case
Of 'carry on regardless', but of 'know
The peaks and know the pits; then know your place!'

Grieve for Me Piecemeal

In memory of Gerhard Koch

Grieve for me piecemeal, dearest, grieve
For what's deleted year by year,
Those bits of self that disappear,
The shrinking self they deign to leave,
The names too far back to retrieve,
Those scenes that fail to show up clear
As each assault grows more severe
And countermands each short reprieve.

It's what goes missing you should mourn,
The gaps that lengthen week by week,
The gist of things now far to seek
In verbal pile-ups, words stillborn,
And every sign that serves to warn
Of what's to come as ciphers speak
Of past lives void, of mindscapes bleak,
Or revenants to silence sworn.

Best take them singly day by day,
Those losses, and refuse to let
Sheer grief for me replace regret
For each thing lost, each new display
Of vacancy. For then you'll pay
No excess price, no outsize debt
Of mourning but, like me, forget
What 'I' and 'me' once let me say.

The coastline crumbles, shores retreat
From hour to hour, and it's for you,
Close-sailing them, to wonder who
Hangs out here, one you might just meet,
Should you put in, and think to greet
Once more had they but met your cue,

Not acted then as strangers do
Who catch your gaze, then cross the street.

Be with me at each stage in my
Stepwise self-grieving but let go
The thought, once we've sat through this slow
Snuff movie, that it's really I,
My one-time self, you've just seen die
When there's no punctual end-point, no
Last flicker of me left to blow
Out gently as you slip from my mind's eye.

Zoom: Four Predicaments

Zoom 1: Tangents

Eyes meet yet who's to know who looks at whom?
No intersect beyond the camera's eye.
All contact distanced in the time of Zoom.

A glance exchanged is too much to presume.
Though sight-lines cross the look goes whizzing by.
Eyes meet yet who's to know who looks at whom?

Those moments in the online waiting-room
Give notice: normal optics won't apply.
All contact distanced in the time of Zoom.

Lean slightly forward and know your face will loom
On every screen, perspective all awry.
Eyes meet yet who's to know who looks at whom?

We yearn to quit this solitary doom
And scan our screens as faces multiply:
All contact distanced in the time of Zoom.

The lockdown lengthens while the networks boom.
Spaced out as ever, but you have to try.
Eyes meet yet who's to know who looks at whom?
All contact distanced in the time of Zoom.

Zoom 2: Dream Session

The faces leap from yellow frame to frame.
We tag along but there's some clue we lack.
Too quick for eye or thought, that catch-up game.

It's not your slow response-time that's to blame;
They zigzag up and down, forwards and back.
The faces leap from yellow frame to frame.

How tell if trains of thought link all the same?
It might be them or us caught losing track.
Too quick for eye or thought, that catch-up game.

Look sharp, be sure your optics take fresh aim
Next time the speaker does a jumping-jack.
The faces leap from yellow frame to frame.

A super-agile mind could maybe tame
The leaps by some neat second-guessing knack:
Too quick for eye or thought, that catch-up game.

Else it's by linking up each speaker-name
With *idée fixes* that Zoom cuts us some slack:
The faces leap from yellow frame to frame.

Zoom-sessions work but how on earth we came
To work them out is what we've yet to crack.
Too quick for eye or thought, that catch-up game.

Still real-world discutants need feel no shame
If jump-cuts force too swift a change of tack:
The faces leap from yellow frame to frame.

Each new screen-memory stakes another claim
To mind-space in our Zoom-decoder's pack.
Too quick for eye or thought, that catch-up game;
The faces leap from yellow frame to frame.

Zoom 3: Delirium

Just switch from 'gallery' to 'speaker view.'
Should sort things out but still you're all at sea.
Switch back to gallery and scan the crew.

Ten minutes in you've not the faintest clue
What's going on or who those folk might be.
Best switch from gallery to speaker view.

It rings a bell, that voice of his, but you
Can't place it — Zoom-induced, that syncope!
Switch back to gallery and scan the crew.

'Surely', you say, 'they've have better things to do
Than crash Zoom sessions all day long — like me!.'
Best switch from gallery to speaker view.

He knows his stuff, gives answers bang on cue;
To you they're code unknown though public key.
Switch back to gallery and scan the crew.

Maybe this thing's a secret rendezvous,
Fixed up to trap one clueless attendee.
Just switch from gallery to speaker view.

Else you're Zoomed-out and your delirium's due
To some great online session-hopping spree:
Switch back to gallery and scan the crew.

If it's the same routine they're going through,
That nonsense-talk, that random *potpourri,*
Then switch from gallery to speaker view!

You say 'Well, call me paranoid, but who
Would host it just to spook one invitee?.'
Switch back to gallery and scan the crew.

Host-guest, guest-ghost: the etymons ring true,
If nothing else, in your Zoom-haunted plea.
Just switch from gallery to speaker view.

Each session brings the crisis on anew,
The panic fear: much better, then, if we
Switch back to gallery and scan the crew.

There in the waiting-room you'll see them queue,
Your fellow-guests, all spooked till they agree:
Switch straight from gallery to speaker view!

Turn video off, let them play peekaboo
With screenshots, wonder whose that lone ID.
Stay switched to gallery and scan the crew.

Then trust Zoom-mania won't too badly skew
Your grasp of things and bring catastrophe.
Just switch from gallery to speaker view;
Switch back to gallery and scan the crew.

Zoom 4: Horizons

No loss, that far-back dream of face-to-face.
Thought thrives the more as social bonds recede.
Why think minds meet where bodies share a space?

Let old-world habits go and you'll embrace
New worlds of thought from body's limits freed;
No loss, that far-back dream of face-to-face.

Mere local prejudice requires we trace
Our bounds with social access guaranteed.
Why think minds meet where bodies share a space?

It's finite but unbounded, that's my case.
Let's not revert to some old space-time creed.
No loss, that far-back dream of face-to-face.

At last you'll find your intellect keep pace
With other minds as they get up to speed.
Why think minds meet where bodies share a space?

A gift, they'll say, for types like you who brace
Themselves for every offline social need.
No loss, that far-back dream of face-to-face!

I say: why grudge us what arrives by grace
Of means to psychic ends so aptly keyed,
Or think minds meet where bodies share a space?

Think rather how their worlds contract who base
Their thought on life's unceasing pressure-feed!
No loss, that far-back dream of face-to-face;
Why think minds meet where bodies share a space?

Exits: Double Whammy

1

Malfunction manifests in different ways.
I see them each decline as time goes by.
My case as well: we've all known better days.

Must be they're entering some final phase;
What else could take the failure-rate so high?
Malfunction manifests in different ways.

Watch long enough and twitch or twist betrays
What's wrong with that quite healthy-looking guy.
My case as well: we've all known better days.

Some fade away, some go out in a blaze,
Some have odd bits fall off until they die:
Malfunction manifests in different ways.

You just have to accept it: mortal clay's
That kind of stuff, so no use asking why.
My case as well: we've all known better days.

Grip slackens, breathing slows, the body sways:
So many sure signs to a practised eye!
Malfunction manifests in different ways.

Not long before a terminal malaise
Conjoins them all and spells 'the end is nigh.'
My case as well: we've all known better days.

You'll find some vital body-part decays
Too fast for all the nostrums they apply.
Malfunction manifests in different ways.

Just time to give your spirits a quick raise.

Distraction helps: why not give verse a try?
My case as well: we've all known better days.
Malfunction manifests in different ways.

2

'The flesh decays but mind and soul endure.'
So Descartes thought, but who'll take that on board?
They self-deceive who think the self secure.

The true believers claim to know for sure.
'Soul-stuff's imperishable, praise the Lord!
The flesh decays, but mind and soul endure.'

It's wishful thinking, that old Christian lure,
A comfort-thought we realists can't afford:
They self-deceive who think the self secure.

'How else but by conceiving mind-stuff pure
And incorruptible is faith restored?
The flesh decays, but minds and souls endure.'

Blind faith: how else convince yourself that you're
In line for that pie-in-the-sky reward?
They self-deceive who think the self secure.

'Think what's left out in your sad life-brochure,
Those hopes betrayed, those griefs and fears ignored:
The flesh decays, but minds and souls endure.'

It's foolish dreams and falsehoods we abjure
Who know full well our lives won't be encored.
They self-deceive who think the self secure.

'You sceptics stay for life's brief overture
But care not how the grand finale's scored;
The flesh decays, but minds and souls endure.'
They self-deceive who think the self secure.

Buckling

Brute beauty and valour and act, oh, air, pride, plume, here
  Buckle! AND the fire that breaks from thee then, a billion
Times told lovelier, more dangerous, O my chevalier!

  Gerard Manley Hopkins, 'The Windhover'

All my undertakings miscarry: I am like a straining eunuch. I wish then for death: yet if I died now I should die imperfect, no master of myself, and that is the worst failure of all. O my God, look down on me.

Gerard Manley Hopkins, 'Retreat Notes', January 1st 1889

Buckle *admits of two tenses and two meanings; 'they do buckle here', or 'come, and buckle yourself here';* buckle *like a military belt, for the discipline of heroic action, and* buckle *like a bicycle wheel, 'make useless, distorted, and incapable of its natural motion.'* Here *may mean 'in the case of the bird', or 'in the case of the Jesuit'; then 'when you have become like the bird', or 'when you have become like the Jesuit.'* Chevalier *personifies either physical or spiritual activity; Christ riding to Jerusalem, or the cavalryman ready for the charge; Pegasus, or the Windhover.*

  William Empson *Seven Types of Ambiguity*

One daily tortures the poor Christ anew
(On every planet moderately true)

  William Empson, 'Earth Has Shrunk in the Wash'

Immortal diamond! So your poems came
Up glinting, spade-struck, levered from the grip
Of God knows what malaise it was let rip
That psychic strife, that tumult of self-blame
So suited to their purpose, those who'd claim
Your soul for Christ at all costs, have you whip
The poem-devil out, bid authorship

A penitent's farewell, and fix your aim
On faith and works. How else but through the stress
Of passion thwarted, instinct blocked at source,
Or the curse heard each time instructors bless
Your spiritual advance — how else then force
The run of words to yield the soul redress
By verse fresh-sprung from rhythm's vaulting-horse?

Let's not blame Bridges if he couldn't guess
What those stretched feet were doing, what strange course
You'd taken, or the covert way remorse
At your perceived backsliding might express
Itself in rebel metrics, doing less
To still the restive soul by sharp divorce
From sensuous appetite than to endorse
That craving through the very restlessness
Of senses held in check. How think to tame
A spirit spurred by every bid to slip
The iambic pulse, by every tongue of flame
Flashed out at daybreak, and by every trip,
Guilt-fed or nature-primed, that broke the frame
Set up for soaring souls with wings to clip.

'Octet for nature, beauty and the call
Of all things dappled, counter, strange, or spare,
While sestet for the sequent call to prayer,
The novice priest new-dedicating all
Those first fine raptures in a Saul-to-Paul
(Though form-accustomed) *volta* placed just where
The sonnet can look back at nature's share
In spirit's Spring yet see its coming Fall
In every quivering leaf.' So they opine,
The commentators, though you'd surely set
Them right on that: no turning-point, no line
To slip across from octave to sestet,
When soul's and nature's languages combine
As letters drawn from God's own alphabet.

How not hurrah their harvesting, their fine-
Drawn instresses and inscapes, all that met
Your eye made wondrous, diamond-bright. And yet,
The life-facts known, who'll not then think the shine
Too harshly rubbed, the Scotist form divine
Beset by Thomist scruples, and regret
Your psychomachia even as we let
Those keen-eyed kennings swiftly undermine
That sense of wrong. No wonder should it 'gall,
Gash gold-vermillion', like your hang-in-air
Windhover, wings outstretched to soar, then stall
And swoop on you, its victim hunkered there,
The stricken Christ caught helplessly in thrall
To God's dark purpose and his own despair.

A prickly issue: how we like to read
Of conflicts, turmoil, madness, all that went
To put us Hopkins-lovers on the scent
Of human sacrifice, yet how we need
To screen it out at just the point where we'd
Be happier if the critics could invent
Some method that might tell us what he meant
Without our having poet-victim bleed
To death before our eyes. Poor Gerard, it's
Your life they've been so anxious to recite
Like a Greek chorus, showing how it fits
Your 'themes' and 'imagery' but not the blight
Of sheer abandonment that often hits
Those cries sent up from depths of darkest night.

Happy indeed the critic who acquits
Himself of all complicity despite
A hawk's-eye view of things that might invite
The charge of relishing the savage bits,
Or torture-worship (verbal thumbscrew-kits
To meet all needs), or whistling from its height
The raptor earth-ward aimed in lethal flight,
Locked dead on target in a strife that pits

'Buckler' against 'buckled.' Though you plead
For our close-reading, still the years you spent
As willing prey to a God-awful creed
Require at least that we not rest content
With glosses on the glories we should heed
And so ignore that grim life-testament.

'Batter my heart, three personed God!': so said
The poet Donne, like you tormented by
Religious doubts and fears yet apt to try
Them out in public, have his conscience read
From lurid scene to scene, and let the dread
Of error and damnation not deny
Him room to get a histrionic high
Off lying in his shroud and playing dead
For godly shock effect. No hellfire-hot
Grand Guignol stuff for you, no great display
Of sinner-saint conversion on the spot,
Just those dark stations of the cross that they,
Your spiritual directors, chose to plot
Lest nature summon and your heart obey.

Yet we your closest readers, might we not
Then find ourselves in league with those whose way
To conquering souls deployed that whole array
Of screw-up strategies for finding what
Best served their purpose, showed the sins that squat
On virtuous lives, then let the priests allay
Their consciences by counting everyday
Griefs and misfortunes something to be got
Well over with their aid? Too soon we shed,
Like your confessors, the connatural tie
Of body-soul and lifeworld that's deep-bred
In your taut rhyme and scansion, felt to lie
Beyond technique and so ensure we're led
To sense, feel, grasp what your words signify.

Yet always there's some turn of metaphor,
Some figural device we might enlist
To mask the terror, hide the zealot's fist
In a glossator's glove, and thus restore
The civil codes of poetry once more
Though predator and prey, like catechist
And novice, stay on target for the tryst
Assigned when living flesh took carnivore
Religion to its heart. See how they screw
Down hard on you, those ministers of fate:
Your parents mortified, the Oxford crew
Suspicious, friends like Bridges apt to slate
Your verse-craft — all who took the falcon's view,
Fast closing in on every fragile trait.

A heart in hiding: no re-casting you
In Donne's role, you so anxious to negate
That restive will, to quell that constant state
Of soul-disquietude they put you through
And keep the conflict strictly *entre vous*,
You and your God, though critics tend to rate
Life-crises by how well they correlate
With all those anvil-hammered poems do
To give that passion voice. It's left to your
Less text-fixated readers to insist
We not join the inquisitors, ignore
The mute appeal, note every striking twist
Of word or phrase yet opt to close the door
On truths too harsh to bear a saving gist.

Villon to Petrarch: a Flyting

She is a paragon to those most perfect spirits,
happy to have changed her residence,
and then from time to time she turns,
looking to see if I am following her, and seems to wait:
so that all my thoughts and desires yearn towards heaven
since I hear her praying for me to hasten there.

   Petrarch, *The Canzoniere*, Poem 346, trans. A.S. Kline

Foolish love makes beasts of men:
It once caused Solomon to worship idols,
And Samson to lose his eyes.
That man is lucky who has nothing.

   François Villon, 'Double Ballade', trans. Anthony Bonner

1

I take your precious verse-forms, twist them round,
And throw them back at you, intact
But minus all the dumb-cluck ways you've found
To keep it up, that lovers' pact!

You Petrarch-prattlers know you're on home ground,
The chat-lines open, password hacked,
And sentiments pre-packaged so you're bound
To get yourselves in on the act.

These days they mostly leave yours truly browned
Right off, those sob-stuff sonnets packed
With courtly-love hyperboles and crowned
By rhymes tin-eared and thoughts half-cracked.

You'll say there's other verse of mine renowned
For stuff like that, with copies stacked

Wherever love's sweet joys and woes resound
Or quick-switch poles repel/attract.

But I wrote best when lady fortune frowned,
When crime supplied the goods I lacked,
So each day I'd make certain to astound
The retailers of scandal-fact.

When things got rough they'd always try to hound
Me down, those rogues in office backed
By royal decree, and each time I'd rebound
With some sweet vengeance to exact.

The pundits would have wagered their last pound
That I'd be hanged, or torture-racked,
Or end my days trussed six feet underground,
My cover blown, my hide-out tracked.

A sobering thought, for sure, but one I've drowned
In wine and wenching till I blacked
My name so deep they started to impound
The reams too risqué to redact.

2

Those fool Petrarchans rage when I lay bare
The ugly truths they strive to hide,
Like ageing bodies, wrinkles, falling hair,
And love turned on its seamy side.

My sin? that I remind them just how rare
And short-lived those delights that I'd
Once brought to life (still can, from my armchair!)
Yet now take licence to deride.

What irks them most is how, for all their care
With courtly diction and their pride
In pillow-talk, it's my harsh music they're
Compelled to hear as worlds collide.

For mine's a world of truths they'd never dare
Come out with, facts too long denied
By every sottish rhymester who'd declare
Petrarch his loony-moony guide.

They rate their mistresses 'beyond compare',
Spread fancy falsehoods far and wide,
And call on heaven to witness when they swear
Death cannot break the knot love tied.

If heaven's listening, just send up a prayer,
Hope some kind angel may provide
A failsafe means of changing foul to fair,
Or trust face-paint and peroxide.

Else you'd best harken to the news I bear
Of faces sagging, squinny-eyed,
Cheeks hollow, pointy noses fit to scare
Kids witless, tear-ducts drained and dried,

Mouths snaggle-toothed, and all the ample share
Of mortal ills the poets tried
To gloss clean over with their special flair
For King-Canuting time and tide.

Coronavirus: Retrospect 2040

It's twenty years ago and more
Coronavirus hit.
It hit the sick, it hit the poor,
And shares went crashing through the floor,
But we said 'wait a bit, you lot,
Stay calm and wait a bit.'

For we saw how this thing might go,
This re-run of old scenes
That pitched the high against the low,
The boss-class guy with loads of dough
Against the might-have-beens, us lot
Of low-class might-have-beens.

We saw it coming, just the same
As when *Titanic* sank,
A life-boat seat booked in their name
But nary a space for us to claim:
We've their class-law to thank, you lot,
Their boss-class law to thank.

The virus had a tale to tell,
A most instructive tale.
It said: I'm here on time to spell
It loud and clear, the future hell
You face if they prevail and plot,
Your fate if they prevail!

A virus is a curious beast,
It's neither live nor dead,
A hybrid thing that, once released,
Has death to bring from 'the Far East',
For that's the fear they spread, that's what
The racist papers spread.

But we got wind of how things stood,
Of what they had in mind,
Those swine who thought 'the common good'
Meant 'you go short, as your sort should;
You're just the common kind, you lot,
The plain old common kind.'

Oh yes, we clocked the message then,
We commoners got the gist:
'They're at their tricks and games again,
Their schemes to fix just where and when
To brandish the iron fist they've got,
That thinly gloved iron fist.'

It's capital that ran the show,
That told us 'listen up:
You paupers may, with luck, pull through
If you'll just pay and join the queue',
But we were sold a pup, that's what —
Us lot were sold a pup.

So listening up taught us to trust
Our wits, not boss-class lies.
It told us how the doubters must
Cease doubting now and deem it just,
The rage that bid us rise, you lot,
The rage that bid us rise!

We knew all crises had a close,
However long they took,
And so it went, as anger rose
And you brave justice-seekers chose
To bring their crimes to book, that lot,
To bring their crimes to book.

First it was 'put all plans on hold
And let the virus run',
Until a graph too plainly told
It might kill half the sick and old:
Who'll hold the smoking gun, big shot,
Who'll hold the smoking gun?

Then they got panicky and tried
To bolt the stable door
With new rules each time someone died,
Though rules whose reach they strove to hide:
They knew the insurance score, that lot,
They knew the pay-off score.

We kicked them out with all their rules,
We kicked them good and hard.
We cleared the land of public schools,
And took in hand the flannelled fools,
And flashed them our red card, you lot,
Just flashed them our red card.

Coronavirus showed the way
To cast their idols down.
It showed how crass the part that they,
The ruling class, had come to play —
The role of licensed clown and sot,
Of corporate-licensed clown.

For there were viruses out there
Ten times more virulent
Since spread abroad by those who'd dare
Have lies and fraud supplant all care
For those they represent — you lot
They claim to represent!

Let's not thank god the virus struck:
It brought us death and grief.
But let's concede that we were stuck,

In desperate need of devil's luck
To turn a greener leaf, that's what:
To turn a greener leaf!

They'd screw things up for good and all,
Those tools of corporate greed.
They'd foul our nest and have a ball
At power's behest or fortune's call
And pay the rest no heed, that lot,
And pay the rest no heed.

Act now, strike back, don't blow your chance!
That's what the virus taught.
Else who knows when they'll next advance,
Through pathogen or high finance,
And bring your lives to naught, you lot,
And bring your lives to naught.

Ruins

Ruins are implicit in every structure.

Roy Fuller

Look close and see the hairline cracks invade.
The finest structures have the greatest share.
Wait till their outlines fade
    and so lay bare
Those artful makings artlessly unmade.

Red Shelley bade the mightiest kings despair
To think how that dismembered hulk betrayed
The brevity of their
    poor masquerade,
Its remnant sand-lashed by the desert air.

The aim precise, the plan minutely laid,
Yet soon they came, those signs of wear and tear
That rapidly conveyed
    how brief and rare
Perfection's joy, how high the tariff paid.

Consult the blueprint, see grain-boundaries err,
The pending wreck in microform displayed,
And most distinctly where
    the highest-grade
Materials vouch a craftsman's utmost care

Time may in time un-weave the double braid,
Send genes astray, entangle some base pair,
And launch a whole cascade
    of kinks to scare
Gene-sequencers tucked tight within their clade.

Some coders say there's back-up code to spare,
Redundant bits to halt the gene-glissade,

While some say 'face it square,
    that endless raid
On all that once declared your course set fair.'

Then we'll suspect the creed we called in aid
As fault-lines grew, the faith we'd scarcely dare
Give up lest doubt so preyed
    on us we'd bear
It with us like a pocket stun-grenade.

Why seek the answer to a loser's prayer
Unless it's in false promises we trade,
Or hopes we might outstare
    the scene replayed
Each time crazed mirrors catch us unaware.

Waves

> *[A man may] ask himself whether his maxim of neglect of his natural gifts, besides agreeing with his inclination to indulgence, agrees also with what is called duty. He sees then that a system of nature could indeed subsist with such a universal law although men [like the South Sea islanders] should let their talents rest and resolve to devote their lives merely to idleness, amusement, and propagation of their species—in a word, to enjoyment; but he cannot possibly will that this should be a universal law of nature, or be implanted in us as such by a natural instinct. For, as a rational being, he necessarily wills that his faculties be developed, since they serve him and have been given him, for all sorts of possible purposes.*
>
> Immanuel Kant, *The Fundamental Principles of the Metaphysics of Morals*, trans. T.K Abbott

1

One wave in parting cost the world to me.
The shoreline trees begin to shake and stir.
Wild branches drive the boats back out to sea.

You say it's offshore wind first shakes the tree
Then drives the boats. Sadly, I can't concur.
One wave in parting cost the world to me.

I too got things your wrong way round till she,
By waving, had them make joint cause with her.
Wild branches drive the boats back out to sea.

'The Sun cast lengthening shadows on the quay.'
Not so: sun-shifters they, the shadows, were.
One wave in parting cost the world to me.

Too quickly we invoke causality,
That pusher-on, that serial *frotteur*.
Wild branches drive the boats back out to sea.

Perhaps the trees alone are truly free,
Their branches swayed as root and sap prefer.
One wave in parting cost the world to me.

For my frail craft their waving holds the key.
The trees command although they shake and blur.
Wild branches drive the boats back out to sea.

'Tack upwind, ride the waves, let tree-lore be!',
Some say, but all their calculations err.
One wave in parting cost the world to me.

Those offshore winds may act, in some degree,
To fix my errant course yet I'll aver:
Wild branches drive the boats back out to sea;
One wave in parting cost the world to me.

2

'An infant stage of thought we've left behind':
Those South Sea Islanders earned Kant's disdain.
When I read him it's them I keep in mind.

He says they're superstitiously inclined,
Lack reason, worship things they can't explain:
An infant stage of thought we've left behind.

And more: when pressed, they offer just the kind
Of pseudo-cause that has them dance for rain.
When I read him it's them I keep in mind.

Mere laziness, he bids us think, combined
With laggard mental powers, their island bane:
An infant stage of thought we've left behind.

That arrogance is chiefly what I find
So striking, so much in the Kantian grain.
When I read him it's them I keep in mind.

If they, the Islanders, strike him as blind
To reasonings *a priori*, then it's plain:
An infant stage of thought we've left behind.

Yet how can he, its votive, have divined
What lay past reason's power to ascertain?
When I read him it's them I keep in mind.

Then I reflect: his every move's designed
To put them down, make out they're barely sane:
An infant stage of thought we've left behind.

He'd have us not let reason's tale rewind
To occult causes, thought deployed in vain.
When I read him it's them I keep in mind.

Boats, branches, that last wave, all intertwined:
Why link them in some one-way causal chain?
An infant stage of thought we've left behind!

The South Sea view: tree, shore and boat aligned
But not close-coupled in causation's train.
When I read him it's them I keep in mind;
'A childhood stage of thought we've left behind.'

3

The bounds of sense are what he'd have us draw.
'Let leafy palms not sink your leaky boat!'
Still branches wave and force-fields stream offshore.

'The starry heavens and the moral law':
These two sublimities got his top vote.
The bounds of sense are what he'd have us draw.

Then what's beyond will serve to conjure awe
And offer thought its needful antidote
Lest branches wave and force-fields stream offshore.

Those folk, like me, made sense of all they saw
In ways that kept their boats and lives afloat:
The bounds of sense are what he'd have us draw.

'Folk metaphysics, thoughts we'd best ignore',
Said Kant, and penned his cautionary note
Lest branches wave and force-fields stream offshore.

Yet how should I, born dryad, not deplore
The schoolbook metaphysics he'd promote?
The bounds of sense are what he'd have us draw.

It's island-dwellers know the causal score,
A knowledge got by heart and not by rote:
Let branches wave and force-fields stream offshore!

So much of life that's unaccounted for
On his account, that stay-home guide he wrote.
The bounds of sense are what he'd have us draw.

Late on his thoughts found South Sea space to soar
In passages the Kant-schooled mockers quote.
Let branches wave and force-fields stream offshore,
Though bounds of sense are what he'd have us draw.

4

No shrewd cartographer but draws a line.
Dragons or risky thought-paths lie ahead!
They choose their risk who plant a no-go sign.

Time was it signalled simply *mine* and *thine*,
Frost's wall, his neighbour's fence, that edge they tread.
No shrewd cartographer but draws a line.

One drawn in sand let Gertrude Bell define
The future stakes for fifty thousand dead.
They choose their risk who plant a no-go sign.

Some beat the outer bounds of the divine
With images to conjure human dread.
No shrewd cartographer but draws a line.

Then those there are, Kant's kindred, who'd enshrine
Truth's bounds as proof of old illusions shed.
They choose their risk who plant a no-go sign.

Mostly it veers from crass to anodyne,
That dull refrain: 'Take care, don't be misled!.'
No shrewd cartographer but draws a line.

My metaphysics: 'up there on cloud nine',
He'd say, 'and (like fake causes) quick to spread.'
They choose their risk who plant a no-go sign.

His borders convoluted, byzantine,
A maze for wary intellect to thread:
No shrewd cartographer but draws a line.

Way up that garden path our worlds combine,
Maybe, but let's not take Frost's point as read:
They choose their risk who plant a no-go sign.

Like hill-crest and rock-layer anticline
Our wave-forms move contrariwise instead.
No shrewd cartographer but draws a line.

Less frequently our two paths intertwine,
Then speed apart like trysts abruptly fled.
They choose their risk who plant a no-go sign;
No shrewd cartographer but draws a line.

5
Each concept-scheme seeks out a world to frame;
Each metaphysic casts its future spell.
Play mind-maps and you play a matching game.

Some moves are major-league: they kill and maim.
What horrors she projected, Gertrude Bell!
Each concept-scheme seeks out a world to frame.

Let concept-schemes affix the latest name
To lands and boundaries that tally well
With mind-maps of the sort that match our game.

So Kant must do his utmost to defame
The dupes of metaphysics who can't tell
Which concept-schemes best marry world to frame.

'Those speculative sorts are all the same',
He says, 'all questing for some place to dwell
Far off the maps whose contours match our game.'

His pared-down metaphysics had no aim
Save coming up with concepts to dispel
The mists that shroud that schema, world-to-frame.

Rogue thinkers, like rogue nations, get the blame
For all that shakes or breaks our concept-shell,
Put up to shield the maps that match our game.

Invade their islands first, then back your claim
With home-grown metaphysics fit to quell
The thought: might they have happier worlds to frame?

Cling to that thought and feel the creeping shame
Of progress gone to pot, the growing smell
Of death given off by maps that match our game.

From North to South, from West to East they came,
Each concept deadly as a cancer-cell
Gene-spliced for folk with other worlds to frame.

No metaphysics without brutes to tame;
No heaven of thought that bears no threat of hell
For those off-bounds on maps that match our game.

145

Schemes, concepts, warships, sun-bombs, towns aflame,
All streamed abroad from thought's high citadel.
What chance for them of happier worlds to frame?
They're dragon-feed on maps that match our game.

6

Thought's empire reaches deep and stretches wide.
Thrice-blest the islander who pays no heed!
Trust none who take Kant's *Groundwork* as their guide.

His ordinances keep the troops supplied
With target happy-spots to meet their need.
Thought's empire reaches deep and stretches wide.

If those exotic types weren't there to chide
They'd have to get the home-guard up to speed.
Trust none who take Kant's *Groundwork* as their guide.

It's lotus-land he dreams up to provide
Some local colour for that white/black creed.
Thought's empire reaches deep and stretches wide.

'No other way of getting them onside,
Those idle remnants of a lesser breed':
Trust none who take Kant's *Groundwork* as their guide.

His moral law's at root what ratified
The pleasure-hater's swift 'no case to plead!.'
Thought's empire reaches deep and stretches wide.

Far better the convicted felon died
For petty theft if that harsh law agreed:
Trust none who take Kant's *Groundwork* as their guide.

'Respecting his autonomy' implied
That death alone could recompense the deed.
Thought's empire reaches deep and stretches wide.

No thought of wedded bliss for groom and bride
But body-parts by contract guaranteed.
Trust none who take Kant's *Groundwork* as their guide.

What wonder should the islanders backslide,
Count pleasures good, rejoice in instincts freed.
Thought's empire reaches deep and stretches wide.
Trust none who take Kant's *Groundwork* as their guide.

7

I feel thought's rule grow weaker day by day.
What islander has trials like mine to face?
It fills my waking dreams, that sunlit bay.

Sometimes I fancy I'm a castaway
On its far shore, amongst an alien race.
I feel thought's rule grow weaker day by day.

My servant Lampe sees his master pray
And still half-doubts my faith but knows his place.
It fills my waking dreams, that sunlit bay.

Why think it's them, not I, who've gone astray,
Who've traded life for some vain hope of grace?
I feel thought's rule grow weaker day by day.

If God's there in his heaven what man can say?
They have their heaven in mortal time and space.
It fills my waking dreams, that sunlit bay.

Just share those dreams and see how I'll betray
Faith's precepts for an island-girl's embrace.
I feel thought's rule grow weaker day by day.

Too long, too long I thought of work and play
As contraries, one virtuous, one base:
It fills my waking dreams, that sunlit bay.

Just hear the keening rise as lovers pay
The price in lives gone wrong to match my case!
I feel thought's rule grow weaker day by day.

Those conjured South Sea mindscapes now convey
What's gone from mine, thought-banished without trace.
It fills my waking dreams, that distant bay.

I know it now: by what migrations they,
Those works of mine, joined empire's paper-chase.
I feel thought's rule grow weaker day by day.

Those island colours shame the grey-on-grey
That fills my sky when striving to erase
What fills my waking dreams, that sunlit bay.

Too late, too late I find the strength to say
What's speakable when words at last keep pace
With thoughts whose rule grows weaker every day.
It fills my waking dreams, that sunlit bay

Sonnet: after Horace

Exegi monumentum aere perennius
(I have made a monument more lasting than bronze.)

Horace, *Odes*, Book III, Ode XXX

Not much to modern tastes, but still applies,
That line of Horace's about the way
A well-wrought verse outlives our mortal clay
And, like words cast in bronze, attains the prize
Tagged not for that which timelessly defies
Time's passage, but for braving come what may
Of upsets loud lamented day to day
By those storm-tossed in free-verse lows and highs.
Less lofty now the message: meanings shift,
Tastes change, their restless motions may deface
The poem like the pyramid; yet still
Its words help stay that Ozymandian drift
Since bearing, faint though legible, the trace
Of thoughts inscribed by intellect and will.

About the Author

Christopher Norris is Emeritus Professor of Philosophy at the University of Cardiff in Wales, having served there as Distinguished Research Professor in Philosophy and, prior to 1991, taught in the Cardiff English Department. He has also held fellowships and visiting appointments at the University of California, Berkeley, the City University of New York, The School of Criticism and Theory (Dartmouth College, New Hampshire), the University of Santiago de Compostela (Spain), the University of Warwick, and other institutions. He has published over thirty books on various aspects of philosophy, the history of ideas, critical theory, and music, as well as having edited or co-edited volumes on George Orwell, Shostakovich, post-structuralism, Jacques Derrida, and the politics of music. His books have been translated into Arabic, Chinese, German, Hebrew, Japanese, Korean, Polish, Portuguese, Serbo-Croat, and Spanish. During his last decade of full-time university employment he wrote mainly about Derrida, Badiou, and topics at the interface between analytic and continental philosophy. At present his work is focused on poetry, poetics, literary theory, and creative criticism.

Photograph of the author by
Valerie Norris. Used by permission.

Lightning Source UK Ltd.
Milton Keynes UK
UKHW012052250821
389453UK00001B/51